TIM

Li T'i-mo-t'ai

TIM CHINA

Li T'i-mo-t'ai

The story of how a Welsh farmer's boy was
instrumental in the modernisation of China

DAVID H. CHAMBERS

Published by David H Chambers

A CIP catalogue record for this book is available from the British Library.

ISBN 978-0-9571589-0-0

Book and cover design by Clare Brayshaw

Prepared and printed by:

York Publishing Services Ltd
64 Hallfield Road
Layerthorpe
York YO31 7ZQ

Tel: 01904 431213

Website: www.yps-publishing.co.uk

Place Names

In the interests of historical accuracy, the names of cities, towns and villages are given as they were at the time of Timothy Richard's life. Place names have had a habit of changing frequently in China as successive administrations have come into power. There has also been an alternative simplified spelling [pinyin] used for some time. Where possible I have put in brackets after the old name, the current usage that may be more recognisable and more easily located.

Timothy Rickard

Contents

List of Illustrations

Preface

It was extraordinary. How many coincidences had to be brought together to create the following?

On May 1986, my wife was driving to work in Oxford from our home in the Cotswolds. Listening to the car radio she passed through an area where the reception was always poor. Pressing the scan button expecting to pick up a local radio station that would give a clearer signal it stopped very quickly at Radio Sussex, a station that had never been received on the car radio before. At that moment a programme interviewing Dr. Gordon White was being broadcast. Speaking on behalf of the University of Sussex, he requested that any relatives of Dr. Timothy Richard contact him immediately as he had been approached by a university in China for information on this man. Pulling the car into the side of the road she just managed to make a note of the contact phone number.

Dr. Timothy Richard was my Great Uncle and this single event, to my mind went beyond the normal bounds of probability by bringing together such diverse variables as location, timing, radio reception and subject matter, it also reinvigorated my interest in this man, Timothy Richard. He was well known within my family due to the fact that he lived the best part of his life in China as a Baptist missionary and eventually married, in China, a like-minded Scottish lady. This unknown Welsh boy, born in a small village in the 19th century was eventually to become one of the most influential figures in forming the modern Chinese nation during the final rule by the "Qing" dynasty and its subsequent transformation into a republic. He impressed his own personality and vision, on an Empire that at the time accounted for a quarter of the world population.

His effect on a changing China and the China as we know it today was profound especially his influence on the application of hygiene, the use of modern medicines and the broadening of education and communication both inside China and to the outside world. It is difficult to envisage that within China around this time there were no railways of any sort in existence – roads were treacherous throughout the year, mainly due to their composition, a windblown deposit of fine grained silt or clay when dry which transformed into a sticky quagmire when wet. He was a trusted intermediary between the West and East even though he was somewhat unconventional – adopting Chinese dress and customs and becoming fluent in many of the local dialects. He adopted a psychological approach to work with the Chinese mind and thought processes – something that was totally alien to most Europeans at that time.

His work also introduced the Chinese to the vast array of European academic works and vice versa culminating in his appointment as Chancellor of Shansi University, a province where some of the most terrible massacres of Christians took place prior to and during the "Boxer" Rising.

So, back to the radio appeal by Dr. Gordon White. The appeal was for any relative of Timothy Richard to contact him to attend the celebration of the One Hundredth Anniversary of the founding of Shansi University. Plans were put in place for me to visit China only to be suddenly curtailed by the events that broke out in Tiananmen Square

Surprisingly some of the later Chinese leaders and influential politicians such as Chiang Kai Shek, were professing Christians and even today there are more Christians living in China than any other country. How did this religious influence come to be so effective? What part did Timothy Richard play in this, how did this person from a rural Welsh background make the journey to the central areas of China, where few Europeans had set foot, become advisor to the Chinese Emperor & protector during the Boxer revolution?

It is remarkable that the name of Timothy Richard is unknown in the west as he was instrumental in helping Central China out of its feudal background and into its first steps of exposure to the developing world. Towards the end of his life, driven home by ill health he died in a suburb of London where only a few people attended his cremation. Had he died in China his funeral would have been marked as one of the most important of any foreigner.

Tanyresgair Farm, Ffaldybrenin 1899

Tanyresgair Farm, Ffaldybrenin 2011

1 – The Making of Timothy Richard

"Europeans would find it impossible to imagine the depths of despair that people went through; driven by prolonged painful hunger they carried out the most atrocious acts that they would never have normally considered. Simply to survive they would release dogs to devour corpses so that they in turn could become the next meal...."

Sitting on a wall in the dry dusty environment of a famine stricken village, the vision of such misery would have stretched the resolve of most ordinary people, especially if they were on their own in a country as far from home and as alien as you could imagine. His thoughts must have turned to the fond memories of the lush green valleys of Wales that he had left several years previous.

In the farmhouse all was hustle and bustle, Timothy had fallen and dislocated his shoulder. The pony and trap were rapidly brought together to take him to the doctors. This really was a rare occasion as usually only his mother and father would ride in this form of transport and the prospect of this excited him so much that he tripped, fell over, and managed to reset the joint. His father gave him a ride anyway to compensate for his obvious disappointment. There were many more mishaps this boy was to get involved in whilst living and working on the farm, some were due to a certain amount of absent mindedness as he drifted off whilst thinking of other things others were due to his natural adventurous spirit.

Later, as a teenager, he would still enjoy the excitement of riding in a pony and trap as it raced along the dusty lanes swaying from side to side as it ran over potholes.

Ffaldybrenin is an area steeped in history and folklore. Its very name translates into King's Fold – born from the tale that Llewellyn, the last of the Welsh princes, had hidden there after being pursued by King Edward. Nearby there is evidence of numerous Roman settlements and industry, the goldmines of Dalaucothu being the last, just surviving into the 21st century. Nearby is the village of Pumpsaint [Five Saints]; and Caio first described in fifteenth century Welsh poetry. Situated between Lampeter, the assize town of Cardiganshire and seat of St. David's College and Aberystwith, it nestles in a green valley at the base of the brown topped mountains where eagles and kites would fly in the empty silence that was typical of this part of Wales.

Timothy Richard, was born in 1845 the youngest of nine children, his father, the local blacksmith and farmer, was also the youngest son of a large family as was his father which meant that he never knew his grandparents. His father was a man of many skills, primarily a farmer and a blacksmith with a good knowledge of veterinary practices, a skill that most of the other local farmers would make use of, he was also the local bone setter and like most blacksmiths of his time a somewhat rudimentary dentist the knowledge of dentistry though being limited to the extraction of teeth. His mother, Eleanor Williams of Llethercoch, Pencarreg was also a daughter of a farmer.

Both parents handed down a store of local lore constantly reciting poems and telling tales and inculcating legends and traditions into the young lad. Previous generations of the Richard family had been farming people or blacksmiths living a simple life with all the associated rural hardships of the time, isolated by today's standards, invariably cut off in winter but bound together by their deep religious convictions and feeling of community. As was usual in those days, families did not move far away and primarily intermarried within the local villages of Ffarmers, Ffaldybrenin, Pumpsaint and Caio, in fact well into the mid 1900's the Richard family were still strongly resident in these places.

When he was five, the family moved to Tanyresgair Farm, just outside Ffaldybrenin. As a youngster Timothy worked hard on the farm helping with the harvests – stacking the straw on the fields, loading it onto the carts and helping to build up the hayricks. Haverfordwest was visited annually when the fair, *ffair wlan*; was held. This time they would set off early in the morning, using the big cart to carry the goods and produce they wished to sell. The route to the market town had added excitement as they travelled between the dark lines of trees and then broke out into clearings splashing through the fords at Trewilym and Dwr Mwntan. Being a country lad he was transfixed by the closeness of the houses in Haverfordwest, towering above him and then there were the clean narrow alleys to be explored, the thronging clatter and chatter emanating from all those around suddenly giving way to a peaceful haven with only the occasional cat or dog to be seen sitting at the open doors of each abode. He daren't venture too far as it was so easy to get lost. It was so different from the countryside. His formative years brought about the usual mishaps associated with young high spirited boys, playing with his friends in the fields and woods unaware of the time of day, arriving home late to be scolded by worried parents. As with all boys he got into scrapes, fortunately without serious injury, Animals surrounded him, the horses providing the working power, the ducks, pigs, geese and pigs the food. He watched the piglets grow up and being slaughtered – their throats cut and the blood collected in buckets for later use, all of this held a strange fascination for the young boy as did his inquisitiveness when looking and poking at the side of a pig that had just been cleaned and salted and was now lying in a trough in the outhouse. He helped to pluck the chickens and chase rabbits, bringing them back for his mother to dress and put in the stew pot. This willingness to work however did expose him to "incidents" in his developing childhood. In later life people were always curious as to how he had been branded with the letter "T" on his forehead. The explanation was quite simple, he had come across his father's horses resting from ploughing and when no-one was looking picked up the reins of the team and urged them on, unaware that they were progressing much too fast for his own safety. Suddenly the plough blade struck a stone which flew up cutting his forehead –leaving that distinctive scar for the rest of his life. When he was eight his father instructed him to keep watch over a horse that was grazing near a hedge – emphasing that he must make sure that the animal did not eat any of the corn. Being a studious boy, Timothy sat down concentrating on his schoolwork for the next day. The horse sensing this lack of attention began to move into the corn and took the opportunity to start eating it, on realising this, Timothy's reaction was to give the horse a sharp slap with his book to move him away but the horses reaction was even quicker, kicking him over a ten foot high hedge, The result – another battle scar.

On another potentially more serious occasion he hadn't come home and was much later than he would have normally been. His brother and father went to look for him and discovered him stuck in mud shouting for help. The joy of finding him was tempered by the fact that he had lost his boots in the struggle to extricate himself but the most significant incident that was the talk of the family for many years occurred when he was twelve and anybody witnessing it would have viewed it with a mixture starting with horror and ending in relief and amusement as the event unfolded. Most of the heat for the Richard household was provided by coal, a mineral that was abundant in the area. The pits were about twenty miles away and his brother Joshua had gone on with a cart and a couple of horses to bring the coal back. To manage the return journey with a full cart, an extra horse would be required to negotiate the hills and Timothy was sent off later with the third horse to meet his brother and then to help add the extra horse at the start of the first steep hill. This third fresh horse was attached without a problem but whilst his brother's attention was diverted [he was talking with other carters] Timothy sought to display his prowess by moving these heavy loads very efficiently and quickly. He started off well ahead of the other carts. All was going fine as they climbed the first steep hill but then the road turned-levelled off- and began a steep descent. Timothy by now had progressed quite a considerable distance from his brother and he decided that rather than wait he would press on downhill. The fresh horse began to pull, and the horses contained within the shafts found it difficult to restrain the wagon with its full load. He went up front to restrain the fresh horse but no sooner had he left that horse to tend to the others than it began to pull again. It was obvious that the situation was dangerous, the horses were now pulling a ton load down a steep hill when they should have been resisting, by now they were trotting which meant that he Timothy, was having difficulty holding back the lead horse whilst trying to return to the coupled horses and use the reins to in a bid to control them from the wagon. Desperately running from one to the other he could see that the position was getting dangerous and that the wagon, swaying from side to side, was now travelling too fast for him to jump from. Fortuitously he caught sight of a tree in the hedge and seizing the opportunity jumped and held on to a branch allowing the horses and wagon to rush underneath and past him. At the bottom of the hill there was a river and beyond that a small village, the inhabitants could hear the rumbling wagon bearing down on them, and looking up, saw the team of horses with a wagon in tow going at full tilt with dust spilling out behind them. At the last moment, as they approached the river, the fresh horse broke free and ran on, its traces dangling until the villagers managed to restrain him. When his brother arrived, the other two horses were stood quietly in river drinking water and what could have been a catastrophic event for all ended with only a few lumps of coal being dislodged but what a tale to tell when they got home!

These rather workaday junior years gradually gave way to the time for education. Most schooling in those days was allied to the church or chapel and in Ffaldybrenin his first schooling was at a day school connected with a Congregational Chapel built in one of the fields on his father's farm. Education was given a very high priority amongst the Welsh country communities and whilst there was no national or compulsory system of elementary education [W.E. Forster's education act was not passed until 1870]. Timothy was fortunate that his father mixed and conversed with many educated people some of who would travel from Lampeter, a seat of learning in those days as it still is now, to discuss religious and philosophical ideas. It should be remembered that the community at large were totally Welsh speaking and these discussions brought Timothy into contact with those that spoke English, his first experience of having to master a second language. This gave him a love of the spoken word and an interest in languages; little did he know that there were many more languages to learn in the future. At the age of fourteen he suspended his education and carried out a years work on the farm, his father wishing him to carry on utilising his skills at ploughing with a team of horses, reaping the corn when ripe, flailing, thatching and looking after the farm animals. His mother and brothers were more in favour of his desire to further his education. As he spent his time tending the animals or scaring crows off the crops he began reading Latin and became acquainted with Greek. Eventually a deal was struck that if his father supported him for one more year he would not ask for any further help from the family and he would become self supporting. He went to a school at Cross Inn kept by his cousin, which was about twenty miles away, to broaden his education. He progressed rapidly. By now he was fifteen and a year later at sixteen he was himself teaching in a mining village, teaching the children at day and the miners at night. This gave him sufficient income to pay for his own further education at the Grammar School in Llanybyther where he again managed to offset the costs by standing in for any master that was absent. He soon took charge of a school at New Inn and then with his savings, supported himself at Swansea Normal School. His brother Joshua, who had generously given Timothy the freedom to further his education also expressed his desire to further his own knowledge and between the two of them they swapped vocations during the winter months so that while Timothy did farm duty Joshua was able to attend school.

It wasn't long before Timothy at the age of eighteen was asked to master at an endowed school at Conwil Elvet. This brought about his first experience of local prejudices when some parents withdrew their children from his tutelage, probably due to his young age and perceived lack of experience, consequently he found himself teaching only twenty-one scholars. Such were his abilities that the school soon prospered and eventually he had over a hundred and twenty pupils under his care. He displayed an ability to bring out the best in his pupils. He approached problem children using a degree of psychology that was way ahead of its time. An example of this approach could be illustrated by one young boy who was constantly in trouble and had problems in relating with other pupils. Timothy took him to one side and making sure that no one else was able to listen to their conversation asked why he was behaving in such a confrontational manner. The lad came out with stock answer that everyone hated him. Timothy, with some gentle probing found that this boy did in fact have one friend who did like him only because as he put it, "He likes everyone". Armed with this knowledge he managed to persuade the boy that if he should also act in a similar manner and try to be friendly and approachable with everyone he too would be liked. He assured the lad that no one else would know of the conversation that they had just had. The effect was better than even he could have imagined, for the previous aggressive nature of the boy contrasted with his change of attitude and caused the other pupils to warm to him quickly so much so that in fact he became the centre for much of what went on the playground and in turn became the leader of the playground gangs, a much more cheerful character – no longer the isolated figure.

His move into the Baptist church was only to be expected with such a strong religious family and community around him. He had been baptised in 1859 in the river near his home along with Fifty-one others. Being the youngest and with the river in full flood his was the first baptism to be carried out that day. Remarkably, it only took six years for him to deliver his first sermon in Salem Chapel. His education had progressed to such a degree, as had his confidence and bearing that the local elders would remember him and speak of his abilities for many years after.

The Welsh have always had a natural love of music and Timothy was no different. He mastered the Tonic Sol-fa, this being a relatively new form of learning music at that time. He introducing it to Haverfordwest College where he was a student in 1866 whilst at the same time expanding his understanding of English in order to further his contacts. During this period he started to become noticed by peers and tutors alike for his instinctive grasp of differing subject matter, although he was not one of he most imaginative or energetic of people, he did spend a lot of his time in deep thought, a trait that drew people towards him. He had a keen interest in philosophy and was driven to expand his intellect by exploring associated problems through delving into theological treatises.

Not being satisfied with improving his English he started to develop an interest in modern languages, especially those of the East. Little did he know that this interest would become his mission in life. He became a prime mover to lessen the exposure of students to the "dead languages" of Latin and Greek at college and promoted the bias towards that of China, India and Egypt. He also expounded the teaching of scientific knowledge which to many staunch religious heads amounted to heresy. There were people spreading new knowledge about the age of planet earth that flew in the face of religious teachings, people like William "Strata" Smith in Oxfordshire & later Somerset, the "Father of British Geology" who's probing of fossils deposited on sedimentary layers led him to establish an evolutionary timescale somewhat different to preconceived religious edicts at that time. This was before the bombshell that Darwin was to drop but even so it caused much searching of beliefs and doctrine amongst his elders.

Haverfordwest had for sometime been something of a crossroads in Welsh culture. Its name was derived from the Viking influence and it was and is perhaps the most "Anglicised" of the major Welsh towns. This area of Pembrokeshire, Cardiganshire and Carmarthenshire were strongholds of the Baptist movement that exploded with religious fervour around this period. This created a dichotomy within academia, for whilst students were promoting the "new order", tests on students and teachers on their beliefs were abolished in 1871. Faced with the willingness of these students to be expelled for their modern thinking, the heads of the colleges rolled over and gave these headstrong young men some freedom in thought and teaching. It was some fifteen years later when he visited his Alma Mater that Timothy found that as soon as he and his fellow reformers had left; the old order had re-established the conventional thinking and abandoned the "new" studies.

Whilst at Haverfordwest Timothy began to further his interest in the Far East. Due to the low literacy skills of the majority of the population most people had never heard of Marco Polo or his exploits in China. This was not helped by the fact that in previous centuries his tales had been regarded as mostly exaggerated fantasy and were only beginning to be appreciated by the larger population when the printed word became more accessible. He immersed himself in the diaries of Marco Polo who had travelled much the length and breadth of China as an emissary of Kublai Khan over a period of some twenty years, he could see the benefit of accessing the millions of people and to expose them to Christian teachings as indeed Marco Polo had done, ostensibly to start developing trade. Polo had also sown the seeds of interest in Christianity in those that held power but he returned to a somewhat sceptical Venetian government who, as stated, regarded some of his stories as fairytales. Marco Polo travelled over much of China and made notes and observations that were not to be repeated or seen again until the 19th century. It is true that he did not record specific items such as the Great Wall nor record the minutiae of everyday life and customs such as women's foot binding, calligraphy or the consumption of tea. Had he done so it would have helped remove the doubt of his rather elaborate tales from within the minds of later travellers. Nevertheless, the parallels of Polo's journeys and experience with that of Timothy are notable. Both had access to the Chinese court, both could speak several languages {although Polo did not speak the native Chinese tongue} and both were captivated by that great land and people.

The catalyst that sprang Timothy's mind and vision towards China was a lecture by a Mrs. Grattan Guinness on the China Inland Mission (C.I.M.) He immediately offered his services as a missionary but was advised that a better route with his background would be the Baptist Missionary Society. He was interviewed and expressed a particular interest in Northern China displaying some quite visionary reasoning that the North, being a more temperate area than the hot south would be an easier place to work allowing him a longer time to meet and integrate with the extremely large population of these regions. This would then allow the area to be a springboard for spreading his missionary work through the remainder of China. He obviously impressed the board because he was asked to pledge that he would not marry for two years if he were to be given the post. He pointed out to the committee that there was as much risk when taking a wife in the new found areas of Africa and since there was no such restriction on those going to that continent he refused to be bound by such a pledge. After a brief return to Pembrokeshire he was notified that he had been successful in his application and in no time found himself at Liverpool waiting to board the Blue Funnel Line ship "Achilles" heading for China, his father having travelled with him to see him off. Whilst waiting in a small hotel prior to boarding he befriended two men. One was an emigrant to the United States of America, who found out that he could not board as he had not received a money order in time. Although not being terribly flush with cash himself, Timothy lent this man the money to tide him over. Unfortunately, although he now knew the name of the man he had given the money to; he had not taken note of the name of the sender. Consequently the Post Office refused payment. He had better luck with the other – a doctor – who was also travelling on the same ship and who paid promptly on arrival in Shanghai.

2 – An Introduction

Before we move on to Timothy's journey to China, it is worth reflecting on the environment he was thrusting himself into. The Chinese attitude to foreigners was, at the best, one of suspicion escalating to pure hatred. It had not always been so and the change of attitude should not come as a surprise considering the way that they had been treated. When Timothy arrived foreigners were tolerated primarily through *force onisab*. If we were to step back to the times when the Romans were occupying Britain, the Han Dynasty was nearing its end but it was also a period when traders from the areas west of China and Buddhist monks from the East were well received and mixed freely with the indigenous population.

In the T'ang Dynasty [618-906], Jews, Mohammedans, Japanese, priests and people from various nations were welcome at court, mixed freely and lived in the capital. The following Dynasties Sung [906-1279] Yuan or Mongol [1280-1367] all encouraged foreign trade and communication. Witness Marco Polo – given access to the court and freely allowed to travel as the Emperor's emissary within China. In the 13th century the Polo family were officially received by Kublai Khan and then sent back with a Mongol guide who was to act as an ambassador to the Pope. It is illuminating that this man called Koeketei took with him a request from the Khan that the Pope should send 100 intellectuals to teach Christianity and educate the Chinese on western customs and ways of life. The Polo's were also given a golden tablet [paiza] which acted as passport and royal warrant granting the holder the right to lodging, stabling and food throughout any journey taken within the Khan's dominium.

The death of the Pope prevented them carrying out this duty and after much delay whilst waiting for the election of a new Pope the Polo family, with the young Marco, together with two monks carried gifts from the Pope and returned to China. During the many years spent there Marco Polo developed a strong relationship with Kublai Khan who in turn entrusted him with several diplomatic missions within the country eventually promoting him to governor for a number of years.

On his return to Europe his tales of the far land led to greater use of the Silk Roads and an expansion of trade. This led to a gradual deterioration of relations with China during the Ming Dynasty [1368-1644] as the advent of the buccaneering culture, ostensibly to carry out trade but using it as a means to carry out robbery, eventually escalated to pillage and rape. This naturally turned the Chinese against the invader. Coupled with the Japanese pirates harrying the coastal regions, the Spanish carrying out wholesale massacres of Chinese in the Philippines, the Portuguese – who had been initially well received in the 1500's – turning to piracy and finally the Dutch invasion of the mainland and the Mongol incursion towards the north caused the Ming Dynasty to effectively bring the shutters down on the rest of the world by extending the "Great Wall of China".

However, explorers and missionaries still tried to carry on with their work. Francis Xavier died attempting to land on the mainland in 1552 whilst surprisingly in 1600 Matteo Ricci was allowed to settle in Peking and founded the first Christian enclave. The Manchu Dynasty ruled for a considerable time from 1644 right up to 1911 and trade from and between the coastal ports did gradually increased. Internally China still held anti foreigner views but Roman Catholic missionaries had managed to secure safe passage and freedom to travel allowing them to set up a sprinkling of churches throughout the land. This unravelled when they tried to set up a papal government independent of the authorised government, *imperium in imperio,* causing them being expelled. Their arrogance and aggressive self-righteous attitude had angered the court to such a degree that priests were forbidden to enter the country and would face execution if discovered. Traders had many obstacles put in their way, some contact was maintained at a diplomatic level with the "barbarians" a term used by the Chinese to describe every level of contact with foreigners. This gradual breakdown of relationships was further compounded by the opium trade, eventually breaking out into full scale war – later to become known as the Anglo-Chinese War.

The English at this time were exploiting the spoils of their empire. Wealth was built up from what were basically criminal processes. Due to the severe restrictions put on foreign trade, the Chinese allowed only one port – Guangzhou [Canton] to be open to foreign commerce with the exclusive license to deal held by a small group of merchants known as the Co-Hong. The British on the other hand had granted a monopoly to the East India Company to operate under a charter from the crown. This company then traded mainly in silks and tea paying primarily in silver. As the Chinese government had banned opium smoking, the British seized the opportunity to export opium to China from India by a roundabout route. This opium was delivered via private firms that had bought the drug at auctions in India, a guise to distance the British Government from direct involvement with the drug. This was done in order to avoid jeopardising the legal trade in tea.

The British were now on a win – win situation. The profits from the Indian opium auctions produced a significant source of revenue for the British Government, tax was then imposed on the imported Chinese tea and on the traders and to cap it all, the silver used in China to buy opium greatly exceeded the amount that the traders paid for tea! In a stroke the British had managed to turn a heavy trade deficit of importing expensive porcelain and artefacts into a massive surplus by dumping a cheap drug onto an ever craving market.

The British Government eventually removed the East India Company's monopoly of trade with China and private firms rushed in to take over the opportunities presented, Jardine Matheson [still in existence] being one of the first to set up a base in Shanghai. This free-for-all coupled with the increasing use of imported opium alarmed the Chinese and in 1838, the Imperial Commissioner – Lin Zesu took action by seizing the stocks of drugs held in warehouses and detained all foreigners in the port of Guangzhou [Canton or Kwangchow]. Rather than sign an agreement to stop this trade the British abandoned Guangzhou, the Chinese in turn stopped all foreign trade and supplies of food and water to the resident foreigners. This culminated in the British sending out an expeditionary force in June 1840. After several skirmishes over the following two years and many British attacks (backed by naval forces) firing on important forts, rivers and coupled with further blockading of their ports, the Chinese capitulated. Under the treaty of Nanjing they even had to pay compensation for the confiscated opium, promising to reopen Guangzhou, cede Hong Kong Island to the British, open ports to foreign trade and to give Britain most favoured nation status. Critically the Chinese also gave up jurisdiction over foreigners in China.

In the 1850's a number of rebellions also took place within China. There were several Muslim rebellions in the southwest, northwest and an anti government rebellion in Nien but the most significant was the Tai-ping rebellion. This lasted over twenty years and cost at least twenty million lives. Coupled with drought and famine the population of China shrank by some sixty million – almost the size of the current population of the UK.

The Tai-ping rebellion, although internal, was significant because of its connection with Christianity and again with the "foreigner". The leader of the rebellion was a Hung Hsui-ch'uan, the son of a poor farmer yet a very promising student. He repeatedly tried and failed in his examinations to join the civil service and was turned down time and time again ostensibly due to his poor upbringing. He ended up having a nervous breakdown. Around this time he overheard a Christian missionary speaking in public and in his unstable state of mind started to have visions about a grey bent over old man. In one vision this old man told him that he was appointed on earth to slay all demons. Hung assumed that the old man was God and that he, Hung, was there to carry out his instructions.

Hung was tormented for several years with repeats of these visions but did nothing about them until he began to study Christianity under the tutelage of an American Baptist minister. Under this influence Hung with his relatives and followers formed a new religious sect – the God Worshippers- and under this guise started to destroy all non-Christian idols around the area of Canton. As famine gripped the country so did the numbers of followers and they gradually formed a military organisation driven by the claim that the Manchu rulers were the primary propagators of demon worship. This ultimately led to confrontation with the government forces and since Hung's followers had managed to build up a considerable armoury from donations from the ever-increasing band of followers they were in a good position to challenge any authority. They were also extremely well disciplined and being fanatical quite willing to die for their cause. The government forces were surprisingly routed. Hung's army occupied Nanjing in 1853 and then attacked Peking [Bejing]. They were eventually defeated during their northern advance, causing them to wheel round and concentrate their attention on the western territories. Holding on to their power in the Yangtse region the rebel army then started to disintegrate primarily due to Hung's increasingly erratic behaviour – he eventually became totally unhinged – ultimately poisoning himself in 1864.

All of this convinced the Chinese authorities that fanatical Christian sects were plotting similar insurrections throughout the country. Further isolation from the barbarians was the only route to be taken.

As Timothy was arriving in China the Tianjin massacre occurred. This had been based on rumours that were running rife through central China of child kidnapping by nuns. The blame was being attached to Catholic missions who were in fact active in bringing in and looking after orphaned or abandoned children. During 1870 the high number of deaths of these orphans increased still further due to disease. Kidnapping was prevalent in China and one kidnapper arrested in Tianjin claimed that he was working for the local mission and was selling children to them.

The French had for some time assumed responsibility for the Catholic missions to China and in order to stifle the rumours that were spreading, the French Consul took it upon himself to force his way into the residence of the local magistrate and confronted him. An angry crowd soon gathered and the consul ordered his guards to fire on the mob to disperse it. This in turn caused the crowd to riot. The first victim was the consul himself then his assistant. Next they turned on the nuns, killing ten of them and finally eighteen more foreigners. Again the Europeans countered by "gunboat diplomacy" – sending in warships, forcing an apology and extracting reparation from the Chinese.

It is clear to see why the attitude to foreigners from the native Chinese varied from hatred to mistrust when the two major influences – opium and the inculcation of Christian religion were so blatantly promoted.

Into this cauldron of prejudice and antipathy walked Timothy Richard. He had to overcome all of this to carry out his calling.

3 – The First Journeys East

He sailed from Liverpool on exactly the same day that the Suez Canal opened, 17th November 1869. This remarkable feat of engineering was something Timothy was well aware of as some four years previous the Grand Canal in China had been mapped by the War Office. Comparison was inevitable. Cut around 625 A.D. it ran from Hangchow to Tientsin – connecting the north with the Yangtse. It was also, at this time, about the same depth and width as the Suez Canal for although the Suez Canal was open to traffic, it could still only cater for those crafts that were light and with shallow draft, mainly flat bottomed sailing barges. Large boats would be not be able to navigate the canal until much later, until its depth and width had been increased. With the establishment of this final seagoing link coupled with the opening of the American Transcontinental Railway a few months earlier it meant that theoretically the world would be circled by the then perceived forms of rapid transport.

Whilst such progress was being made in the northern hemisphere the centre of darkest Africa was still being explored and most of the Chinese population outside the main ports had still to see a European.

Due to the restrictions of the canal the steamer "Achilles" of the Blue Funnel Line took the traditional route around the Cape of Good Hope. Timothy arrived in Hong Kong, an exciting and bustling city even at that time as was his next destination, Shanghai. During this period of travel between the two great seaports he had learnt all of the 214 Radicals – a necessary requirement, as they are the index to the hieroglyphics that constitute the written Chinese language. Without this key it would be impossible to read any Chinese literature.

Reaching Shanghai on 12th February 1870 he was greeted by the Rev. James Thomas a minister of the Union Church who found him an hotel to stay in for two weeks whilst at the same time giving him open house thus enabling him to accustom himself to the new environment and the strange food but also offering him the opportunity to converse on local topics.

Shanghai at this time was a busy jostling city divided into three sections. These comprised the United Kingdom [International], French and the old Chinese Walled City. It was a treaty port i.e. one that was open to foreign trade by agreed signed treaties following the First Opium War [1842] and the Arrow War [1860]. The Treaty Powers around this time were:– Austria – Hungary, Belgium, Brazil, Denmark, France, Germany, Great Britain, Italy, Japan, Mexico, Netherlands, Norway, Peru, Portugal, Russia, Spain, Sweden and the USA, all with a small foothold on the mainland.

What impressed Timothy about Shanghai was the commercial activity in the American settlement at Hongchew [Hongkew] and especially the buildings along the British Bund a magnificent retaining wall stopping the fast flowing Yangtse from eroding the banks near which a long line of imposing private and public buildings had been and were being built. All of these were situated on broad streets that ran from the Bund to the boundary.

Next to the British area was the French, smaller and somehow darker and dominated by the rather plain Catholic cathedral. Around this building were the Consulate and Town Hall. The French ran their concession on different lines from the British, constantly stoking up trouble by treating it as a colony rather than a settlement thereby causing any number of flare ups to occur with Chinese Government.

In the middle of these concessions stood old Shanghai – a particularly unsavoury area to the European. A wall over three miles long pierced by narrow gateways surrounded it and beyond that a ditch about twenty feet wide and then ramshackle housing going down to the river – a sharp contrast to the stone buildings in the western concessions.

Through being less truculent towards the Chinese, the Americans had gained most favoured status, not so for the French and British who had to gain their privileges by treaty. The French, Portuguese and British nevertheless were still the main trading nations.

Within two weeks he was off again to Chefoo [Yantai] in Shantung Province – a three-day boat trip. Here he met his future colleague Mr. Laughton.

Although Timothy was the virtual founder of the Baptist mission in China, he was by no means the first Baptist. The ports and coastal areas were becoming used to Europeans. Some ten years previously an evangelical society had based itself in Shanghai but with limited funds available two of these members decided to join the Baptist Mission. They to relocated their base to Chefoo [Yantai] as this was the centre of scholarly learning – Confucianism and Mencuisanism. These two, Dr. C.J. Hall and the Rev Kloekers had been to China before and were familiar with the language but within a year Hall had died from cholera and Kloekers was forced to return to England due to ill health.

Mr. Laughton
Before this a Mr. M'Mechan, Kingdon and Laughton had joined them but of the five only Laughton was there to meet Timothy. Disease was the biggest problem for any visitor and within four months Typhus had claimed Laughton leaving Timothy to administer his teachings alone.

During Laughton's funeral the sound of gunshots rang out heralding the next problem for the foreign visitor. A few days previously a massacre had occurred at Tientsin in which the French Consul, his wife and twenty-one nuns were shot or killed by sword. Anti foreigner feeling was running rampant in the region. Timothy must have felt very isolated as the foreign communities were small and spread thinly along the coast —mostly at the large seaports. Communication was not easy, there was no telegraphic system. The only means of contact was being carried out by the few coastal steamers that plied their way north to south. From these it was possible to glean the information that those elements that were foremost in fermenting the massacre were also stirring in several areas.

Now on his own, Timothy immersed himself into learning the language – this he considered his best form of defence should he ever be faced with a potentially difficult situation. In December, Dr. William Brown an Edinburgh graduate joined him and together they started to expand the medical care side of their missionary work. Together they had to overcome the Chinese inbuilt hostility to "The Foreigner". Laughton had left one important legacy – Mr Ch'ing – a Christian convert who became Timothy's assistant.

He set out on a book-selling journey with Dr. Brown, On the very first day Brown's horse suddenly threw him and bolted. Chasing the loose horse and overtaking it, Timothy grabbed the runaway around the neck; the horse then gradually began to draw itself away. He was now in a precarious position with his arms around one horse and his feet on the back of the other. Being a large, agile and strong man he eventually managed to coax both animals back under control. On reflection he realised that this episode could have seen the termination of his activities in China, it also reminded him of childhood experience with horses in Wales.

Robert Lilley

Further journeys took place to sell books and eventually a member of the National Bible Society of Scotland –a Mr. Robert Lilley – who had been in China much longer than Timothy, joined him on Brown's departure. Exposure to danger was still regarded as part of the normal working pattern. Together they decided that after covering the Shantung promontory in 1871 they would complete a number of trips around Chefoo. Having done four trips they thought the next goal would be to venture forth through Manchuria to the borders of Korea. This was virtually unknown territory to westerners as previous intrepid explorers had inevitably been killed, due to the locals' assumption that they were the advanced parties for a larger invasion to be carried out by "strange looking men". During this trip they narrowly escaped capture by brigands [bandits] and on the journey to Manchuria their German sailing ship got caught in a storm, was driven onto rocks and wrecked. Struggling on to the shore they were faced with monsoon rains and could not make any further progress for two weeks. To make any sort of movement they had to resort to travelling by road in conditions that were rendered virtually impassable due to the mud in the area being of a particularly pernicious mix of fine soil [Loess]. The Chinese regarded this soil with some awe as it appeared to come out of the sky. It has since been found that it is in fact windblown sand. The fine dust taken up to the ionisphere from the western deserts – in summer a light brown dust but when wet turning into a paste some two foot deep that stuck to your feet making the withdrawal of each step from the sticky mess difficult and tiring. Again it took Timothy back to the last time he experienced this – as a young boy on his fathers' farm when he lost his boots in the mud!

At least three carts were loaded with bibles and bedding. Each cart had two mules and the two men each had an assistant. Although the ground was a quagmire the heat was intense the sun blazing. Timothy suffered sunstroke. With a severe headache he could not simply lie down in the cart as he and any contents on board were thrown from one side to the other. Lilley took him by the arm and they trudged through the mud some thirty miles to Newchang [Yingkou] where they managed to find somewhere to rest. One of the chests carried contained medicines and Lilley decided to treat Timothy with laudanum. By now he could not open his eyes due to the pain he was suffering. The problem Lilley faced now was that in all the turmoil he had lost the dosage book. Neither of them could remember the correct amount and Lilley sat with Timothy in case he lost consciousness. Luckily next morning he awoke completely revived and years later he read in *The Lancet* that the best cure for that ailment was in fact a stiff dose of laudanum. To avoid a repetition of the problem he covered the top of his head with a pillow for a few days. This form of dress caused much amusement to the Chinese but nowhere near as much as Lilley's pith helmet of which an incredulous audience simply couldn't understand. "Why would a man want to parade himself with a wash basin on his head?" they said. They learnt that a previous missionary used to amuse his audiences by juggling with his glass eye and playing tricks with his false teeth.

Eventually they reached Mukden, the capital of Manchuria, being one of earliest foreigners to visit the ancient centre. As they progressed further to the east they were led to understand from the locals that bands of bandits were loose in the countryside. One night their helpers woke them with the news that mounted bandits were nearby and had occupied an inn further ahead. Their two Chinese helpers were now quite frightened and requested to return at once to Chefoo [Yantai], Lilley and Richard sat down to plan their next move and told them that the two of them would not consider turning back but would offer their helpers their travelling expenses to return. This was not what the helpers expected and faced with the situation of having to strike out back on their own they then rather bravely decided to stand by their masters. At this point Lilley & Richard had also decided to divide their money equally between the four of them lest any one of them were captured. This was not as simple as it seemed as the currency was in the form of silver ingots each weighing about two and a half kilos.

The ingots were taken to a local smithy who heated up the metal, hammered it into thin slabs and then cut it into small squares weighing around thirty grammes, these squares were then sown into their clothing. Weighed down with the currency they started on their journey just as the sun was setting.

As they progressed along the road they noticed that everyone else was going in the opposite direction armed with pikes, staves or farming implements. Eventually their guards came running back to them shouting that the there was a gang of bandits around the next corner. Approaching the bend they could see some tents and then about eleven men moving towards the very inn that they were heading for. It was obvious that the bandits would cut them off before they could reach the inn, so the decision was made to turn round and seek shelter in a farmyard that they had sighted about half an hour earlier.

The farm was owned by an old lady who came to see them and was astonished when the two men spoke in her native tongue. She gladly offered to hide their carts until the robbers had passed. She then sent her daughters out to call the reapers in from the field to come and act as guards and lookouts until the robbers had gone.

The main crop grown around the farm was millet, a tall grass with fronds containing thousands of small seeds hanging down from the top of the ten-foot tall plants. This provided perfect cover for robbers and it also deadened the sound of the horses' hooves until they were very close. Suddenly the bandits broke clear of their cover, their heads covered with brightly covered scarves trailing behind them as they converged on the two men standing at the gate. The sight of two strange looking men dressed in European costume brought them to a sudden halt which soon turned to panic as they were convinced that they had come across the devil and his follower. Shouting that they had just seen such an apparition they fired warning shots to the rest of the band and turning tail disappeared back into the millet plantation. Although Timothy and Lilley had been given revolvers at the start of their journey, they were not inclined to use them, after all they were there to save men, not kill them, so they hid the guns in a convenient heap of straw. They could now hear the robbers regrouping and watched as they rode up again, this time with much more bravado and more heavily armed. What appeared to be their leader was at their head and shouting that he had heard about these "foreigners" and that he recognised them as such. Assuming that they could not be understood, asked his band of men how they should treat the two of them. Turning towards them, Timothy spoke clearly in their own tongue letting them know that they could be understood. This totally surprised the leader, who promptly demanded to know why they were there.

When told that the two of them were there simply to sell or give away books he was even more incredulous and simply could not believe that they could possibly do any trade with an uneducated population, his scepticism gave way to amazement when they pulled back the covers on both carts to reveal stacks of books.

They then slowly opened the farm gate and took several books out to the band of armed bandits, all of whom were still mounted with their firearms cocked. It became evident that none of the bandits could read. Thrusting the books into their hands they could see that the robbers were getting increasingly nervous, they were still not convinced that they were not seeing the devil and were visibly shaking with fear. To help them relax they offered them more books to take to their friends – these too were declined. To defuse the situation the leader came forward and explained that their anxiety stemmed from the stories that they all had heard of strange looking men travelling through the country but this was the first time they had seen any and they were naturally curious. The leader then begged the two men not to pass on to the authorities any knowledge of this encounter or of their whereabouts; firing two more shots into the air they wheeled round and disappeared back into the swaying millet fields.

This now left the two in a bit of a dilemma. If it became known in the area that "foreigners" were around then they were going to be terribly exposed with little or no protection whilst at the same time they dare not break the verbal promise and trust made to the brigands not to indicate their whereabouts. It was evident that news travelled fast from village to village. They also found that their "peculiar" form of dress was quite accurately reported in the local areas where they were seen but gradually became grossly distorted further afield as the accuracy of the word of mouth descriptions became ever more vague – eventually they found out that they were being described as "Devils", hence the anxiety whenever contact was made. Further distortion was evident when they entered a small town. Lilley went on ahead with the carts to find an inn while Timothy set up a stall to sell the books. The first thing he noticed was that the streets were empty and the doors and windows boarded up. Walking past one house he peeped in and saw that it was occupied, and stopping, he called through the door to see if anyone would like some books. The occupants immediately scurried through and out of the back door. Just as Timothy was returning to his books, he saw one man very cautiously, approach him and then – in a short while later – a further group behind him who were clearly trying to offer some form of protection to their leader. Timothy managed to convince the man and his followers that they had nothing to fear from him and a small crowd soon gathered round gaining confidence as they spent more time talking with him.

The time then came for Timothy to catch up with Lilley and on his way to the inn he noticed that the locality had changed from being one similar to a "Ghost Town" to one alive with armed men with sentinels stationed at every corner. They immediately settled into the Inn having been offered the best room – known as the mandarin's room. Further inspection showed that the other rooms had damp floors, some had puddles but they all backed onto the pig sty.. The beds, needless to say, were crawling with all sorts of vermin. The walls were black and slimy with the remnants of some decorative paper hanging down and containing all sorts of creepy crawlies. But the mandarin's room was different. It had a high roof boarded floor and a paper window. They went through to the open "restaurant" fitted with rough benches and tables where they had their evening meal and as a matter of course went outside to check that the carts and mules were secure. Shots suddenly rang out and with bullets flying through the air and past their heads they dived into the straw bales to seek cover. Deciding that the situation was too precarious for both of them to be unguarded they took it in turns to watch over their possessions and mules. During his session Timothy dosed off and on waking up looked through a hole in the wooden bay separating them. Convinced that someone was making off with mules he jumped up shouting a warning to Lilley and as they both ran round the bay they discovered that it was actually only one mule going round in a circle grinding corn and not several passing their spy hole.

Next day they sat down with the innkeeper and asked why everyone in the village was armed. He told them that the rumour mill had been going on for some time in which it was said that the "Devil Robbers" would put on European dress and ride in and plunder the small communities, a fact that had gained credence when recently nearby, armed bandits had descended on the town on the pretext of looting the Christian church only to turn their attention to the much more profitable aspect of looting of the whole town.

This rumour now went ahead of them and at their next planned stopping place every inn refused them admission forcing them to rely on their native helpers to go on ahead and secure accommodation. At the next inn, they tried to get into their rooms without being noticed but the landlord suddenly appeared and sizing up the situation, decided to round up all the remaining guests and servants and barricade themselves in the main room. To defuse the situation, Timothy shouted through the makeshift barricade that they had nothing to worry about, as he and his companion would sleep outside in the carts. The night-time temperature now rapidly dropped and a frost started forming. After a couple of hours one of the guests came round the barricade and suggested that he would share his room with them. They were both only too pleased to accept this kind gesture especially as they could now sleep on a K'ang – a brick built bed occupying almost half the room but heated underneath with a fire. This form of comfort was common in Northern China and the fire was generally kept going throughout the four winter months.

Further problems arose at their next stopping point – Sa Ur Hu – an ancient Manchu fortress. The inn they were staying at had clearly been the local jail at one time as it still had the shackles on the walls. The following morning Timothy went to the square to explain to the gathering crowd the reason for his visit. He was not a small man but even so a great bull of a figure armed with a horsewhip emerged shouting and cracking his whip, driving the crowds back with each snap and flick of the cord. Timothy did his best to reason with the hulk when suddenly out of the melee emerged a mandarin resplendent in his full brightly coloured silk costume. Timothy took the opportunity to show the mandarin a copy of the Imperial edict which allowed him to carry out the duties he was performing the somewhat aggressive attitude towards him then changed and in complete contrast he was then treated with extreme courtesy so much so that the next day six mounted soldiers appeared and informed him that they had received instructions to offer both men protection in the region. Richard and Lilley got on so well with their new guardians that they eventually volunteered to help to sell the books at each stopping place. When they reached the end of the mandarins' area of jurisdiction both parties were sad to say goodbye.

The Manchurian region that they were in was very fertile with vast expanses of lush grass and vines. Fruit trees overflowed with their produce falling and rotting on the ground. Manchuria was divided from Korea by the river Yalu [Amnok in Korean] that over time had deposited rich fertile amounts of silt from the seasonal flooding. Timothy was probably one of the first Britons to set foot in this area and immediately noticed that whilst the Chinese side of the river was overflowing with produce the Korean side was starving, with children being sold in order to obtain food. To Timothy the reason was obvious – a total lack of infrastructure – the roads were virtually impassable for the greater part of the year and when they could be used they were in such poor condition that they were almost beyond capability of use by anything other than mules or oxen.

At the important border city of Feng Huang Ch'ing stood the Great Korean gate through which the main route leading out of China passed. By previous agreement between the two countries a neutral "no man's land" strip of about twenty miles wide had been established. This had now become occupied by what can only be described as a "Chinese Robin Hood" and his band of about 600 followers. This leader, called Liu Ch'ing K'ai was a popular ruler of this area with the population bringing any complaints or disputes to him for settlement, rather than go through the official channels that were often too corrupt and located far away.

His popularity did not detract from the fact that he was to all intents and purposes a bandit and consequently had to be treated with caution. When the two men approached the Korean Gate they had already witnessed large groups of soldiers of the Chinese Army assembling outside the city getting ready to attack Liu's men.

As they camped by a stream a local Chinese appeared and pointed out that there were two horsemen on the adjacent hill. These were Liu's scouts and his men were in the next valley. Faced with the prospect of being caught between the two warring factions, they decided to up sticks and turned towards Newchang and then headed back to Shantung.

4 – Order from Confusion

One of the difficulties of carrying out any sort of business in China at this time was establishing an agreement for any financial transaction. Currency over a large area of the country was not uniform or controlled. The American Dollar was the favoured means of exchange around the seaports, but to the north and inland, copper coins or silver were used – the silver value being judged by weight whilst the copper coins had a variable value. These coins were called "cash" the term now used generally in western banking. Unfortunately the exchange value of cash varied from town to town by as much as a factor of ten, this was further compounded by a discount applied to bank bills varying from ten to thirty per cent and the popularity of the Mexican dollar at another rate of exchange! This was further compounded by the fact that Chinese currency [the tael] varied in value from town to town.

It was small wonder then most transactions were carried out using silver, the country areas were still waiting for the introduction of paper money.

Timothy now had to plan how he was to carry out his missionary work to, a not surprisingly, suspicious populace who already held their own beliefs, traditions and classical education. He finally decided after much thought that his best approach would be to engage with those that held some influence in the social structure and were recognised and respected not only for their intellect but who were also open to philosophical discussion.

Hearing of a man who fitted this profile, he sent a request, as was the Chinese custom, to call on him at his home. Within no time he had received an invitation to visit. The man, a wealthy salt manufacturer, owned a large area on the coast where the seawater was channelled into shallow concrete lagoons and allowed to evaporate. Salt was a government monopoly and they would fix the price and then arrange transport all over the country thereby making vast profits to fill the national coffers. Timothy was made most welcome by his host who insisted that he had dinner with him. After the meal the merchant took Timothy to an inner sanctum – spotlessly clean – where he worshipped every day. Timothy had brought with him a Christian hymnbook from which he briefly described the contents. After a brief perusal, the host then surprised Timothy by telling him that his sect used one of the hymns contained within the book regularly when they worshipped but he was unable to say how or where the hymn came to be incorporated into their ritual. At the end of this most illuminating day his host insisted on taking him back to Chefoo and they both said farewell, never to see each other again. Elated at this first meeting Timothy decided that it was not prudent to follow it up due to his lack of a full understanding of the language, customs and religious history, he had only been in the country two years and felt it would be insulting if he imposed any claims of greater knowledge on his acquaintances.

Annual fairs were held in temples throughout China where the local population would gather to worship & celebrate. He decided to visit one such fair in the market town of Lung Shan. This town was at the base of a mountain on which was built a very important temple. As he rode into the town he was totally ignored by the locals and, when he attempted to get accommodation, found that none of the inns would admit him. He sat disconsolately on a stone slab in the street, holding on to his pony's reins. Soon, the usual curious crowd surrounded him. One man stepped forward and asked if he wanted his horse fed. Timothy said he did but didn't know where to go. "Leave him with me and I will see to it" was the reply. Trustingly, Timothy handed the man the reins and the horse was led away. Then another man this time wearing a grease stained apron – a clear sign that he was a cook – approached and said that his master had sent him. Having heard that none of the inns would put him up, he wanted to offer him somewhere to eat and sleep. Naturally this was gratefully accepted and when he arrived at the house he found that the owner was a very influential man in the area, his great grandfather having been governor of the province. On settling in Timothy was told that the fair would not to be held for another two weeks but that he was welcome to stay for whole period.

This official had two sons, both of whom were studying for their degrees in university. Fortuitously they had a thirst for knowledge, especially that of the outside world. They soon gathered for discussions and gradually the discussion group grew as the two sons brought in local academics and teachers eager to find out about foreign civilisation and religion. Timothy gained as much from this as they did and with the boost to his confidence and a new insight to into Buddhism he asked the local priests' permission to speak to the crowds of people that had gathered at the temple. On the day of the fair the temple was swarming with worshippers as well as people buying and selling and as he walked to the centre more and more people pressed close to him, anxious to have a look at this "curious" foreigner. Eventually he was swept along to the temple where he managed to find a vantage point to see and be seen. He watched procession after procession pass by with each village group banging drums and waving banners making as much of a spectacle as they could and increasing the volume of the noise with gongs and cymbals where possible. The air was thick with the smell of incense as each one in turn burnt their offerings, bowed before their idols and backed away. By mid-day the cacophony abated as each village had now paid its respects. This gave Timothy the golden opportunity to stand on a platform and address the crowds who were eager to look and to listen, mostly out of curiosity. Afterwards some did come forward and invite him to visit their villages. Elated at the success of this, it would be some time before Timothy would come to realise that this was not the most effective method of carrying out communicating his work.

He remained firm friends with the father and his sons for the rest of his time in China. Each would visit one another whenever Timothy was in Chefoo.

It was not long before Timothy had the urge to travel into the interior. Chefoo by now was rather overrun with missionaries of all persuasions and he felt that he had to get in first by travelling to areas that had not received the "benefit" of western teachings. He succeeded in hiring a house in a city some twenty miles inland called Ninghai an area not known to have any concentration of missionaries.

It didn't take long to find out why this was the case; there was extreme hostility amongst the governing bodies to any form of "outside" influences and they had successfully manipulated the local lawmakers so that they created as many obstacles as possible for any missionary to enter the interior.

Timothy's landlord was arrested and thrown into jail – a typical example of the methods employed. The poor man resorted to writing to Timothy begging him to help save him which gave Timothy no choice but to escalate the issue to the British Consul. This in turn resulted in a letter which Timothy was told to take to the Ninghai Magistrate. On receipt of the letter, the magistrate asked Timothy to visit him to discuss the matter, coincidently during the ensuing meeting a group of city elders happened to arrive with the intention of making a deposition that no houses should be rented to foreigners. All Timothy could do was refer the magistrate to the agreements and treaties already in place between England & China and point out the importance of the Consul's letter. As he walked back to his house he was subjected to much barracking and verbal abuse and at some time during the night excrement was plastered over the entrance of his lodgings. He now decided that he would not ask for the pursuance or punishment of any the offenders as he was increasingly concerned about his landlord who was still locked away in chains. He decided that his only route out was to leave quietly in the hope that no further actions could be taken against any party. Having received an invitation to visit two Buddhist monks in a neighbouring village gave him just the excuse he was looking for. As a result of this visit further people joined them and a philosophical discussion took place on several aspects of Christianity, Taoism and Confucianism. This further led on to a discussion on the practice of sorcery and the effect of superstition on communities within the different areas.

On Timothy's return to Chefoo he mulled over the attitude of the Chinese to these issues and decided that much could be gained from demonstrating and lecturing on suitable experiments within the subjects of physics and chemistry. This, he felt, would give the Chinese a better understanding of the wider modern world.

Such were the stirrings of ideas in Timothy's mind – a broader education on natural philosophy, the importance of good communications – that the first steps to the foundation of Shansi University were starting to be mentally formed.

University education in China at this time was based around triennial examinations for the M.A. degree [Chu-ren]. Before the candidate could sit for these he had to pass two previous ones, the first being a District examination for which no degree was given and the second was for the Prefecture. A prefecture could contained several districts [hseins] with a population amounting to several millions. From this examination out of a total of perhaps three thousand candidates only about a hundred could expect to proceed to a third and final examination at the provincial capital Chi-nan-fu which was in Shantung province and at the time had a population of over sixty million people.

It was now 1873. Timothy with Lilley and Mr M'Intyre happened to visit Chi-nan-fu during these examinations. The journey from Chefoo took ten days to cover the three hundred miles and this was in fairly good weather. The roads again, being in parlous condition. When they arrived the city was heaving with the influx over twelve thousand extra people, some being competitors for the degrees others being teachers, supporters and of course family and friends. Out of this mass only about a hundred would emerge with the coveted civil degree and a similar number for the military degree. Since there had been hostility shown to foreigners at a similar gathering for civil degrees in Hangchow, the three men thought it would be a little more pragmatic to mix with those students who were competing for the military and with whom they knew they could assimilate easily.

The time came for Timothy's two friends to return to Chefoo, as he had opted to stay on for winter.

The mixing with the military students did bear fruit when a lieutenant under his teaching decided to become a Christian. Around the West gate of the city were three springs spouting great geysers of warm water and prized for their healing qualities. It was in the lake formed from these springs that Timothy baptised him. This spectacle of two men on a cold winter's day walking into the warm water fully clothed naturally drew a crowd of spectators – the Lieutenant stood steaming in the cold air and explained to the crowd the meaning of the rite. Several waited to have further discourse on the subject.

During his time in Hangchow and Chefoo it was apparent that the German influence was quite strong in the area with protestant missionaries plying the coastal routes by boat. You will recall that he was on board a German vessel when it ran aground earlier on his trip to Korea. The Germans were mapping the area around Peking in the early 1800's. Mohammedanism was also to be found in scattered communities in the east and naturally had a stronger hold in the west. At this time there were two large mosques in Chi-nan both with a large following. When in the centre of Hangchow he met two other missionaries, both American. One McIlvaine was a scholar who was the first to publish literature for the Moslems in the country, the other, Crosset, was a kind man who gained many friends. Unfortunately being the only Europeans, the loneliness, coupled with the often hostile surroundings eventually drove both of them insane. Crosset returned to America but McIlvaine unfortunately attached himself to Timothy which caused him more problems than he really wanted at this time due to his irrational behaviour and peculiar dress sense – it was neither Chinese nor European and was made from some obscure animal skins. The Chinese mocked and tormented him to such a degree that he had a total breakdown, gave up his calling and he returned to Chefoo to become a teacher where presumably his eccentricities were masked by his new vocation.

The story did not end there with Crosset. Arriving in America he submerged himself in the study of obscure religious sects. He still craved to work in China but his mission would not allow him to do so. He became a crewmember on a boat in San Francisco and worked his way round to the Holy Land. On his way to Jerusalem he chanced to meet the Roman Catholic Bishop of Chefoo. Spurred on by this encounter he worked his way to

Bombay and again boarded another ship as a crewmember and arrived once more back in China.

When he eventually got to Chefoo, his old friends could not believe how unkempt, smelly, dirty and ragged he looked. They bathed him, fed him and gave him new clothes and a room. He refused any gift of money and when his friends hid some in his coat pockets, he gave it away to the first beggar he came across. He then walked the three hundred miles to Chi-nan, treating the sick as he went, and on arrival his friends there were once more shocked at his appearance as he had done nothing with himself, but nevertheless they too were overjoyed at seeing him again.

He eventually ended up in Shanghai his health broken. Convinced that the air on plains of Mongolia would assist his recovery, he boarded the S.S Eldorado for Tientsin, the captain having given up his cabin for the obviously sick man. He died on route and Timothy who was away at the time returned to place a stone over his grave.

5 – The Second Journey

A greater part of missionary work in China involved medical care, this being seen as part of the whole, the remainder being teaching and praying. By these means the various Christian missions hoped that they could influence individuals and communities to adopt their faith. The Chinese were already immersed in their own methods of healing which primarily were based on herbal remedies. This form of diagnosis and subsequent treatment had not changed for hundreds of years and the death rate in China was comparatively high with endless waves of typhus, typhoid, dysentery, cholera etc. Most of these went unchecked due to the closeness and density of the communities and also due to the lack of sanitation and total ignorance and perception of how these diseases are spread.

Small-pox was, quite rightly, looked upon with fear, not for the consequences of the disease, but for the fear of offending the god that scattered its effect. Its name in China was "divine flowers". A name given so as not to offend the god responsible, the goddess had to be worshipped consistently to ensure cure or removal of the curse from the area. The need for isolating those infected to prevent the spread of the disease was never considered it was treated in the same way as measles. People would mix with those who were infected, if they caught it and survived then they were immune from then on. A pockmarked bride was looked on as an asset – the husband would not be faced with the cost of an early burial or another wedding. At the time half of the population would die from the effects of this one disease alone.

Timothy had now left Chefoo and based himself in Wei-hsien. Previously M'Intyre had rented a house there and the usual anti foreigner feeling arose with mobs gathering outside the house. Fortunately, one of the local gentry arrived and told M'Intyre not to be alarmed, as he would declare his support for him. It transpired that this man a few years earlier had been in Peking when Dr. Lockhart had arrived claiming to be able to control smallpox. He visited the doctor who described and then demonstrated the process of arm-to-arm vaccination from the pustules of a vaccinated person. This process was then repeated again and again with the result that in the area, the disease showed a remarkable decline. To show their gratitude the local people collected sufficient funds to place a plaque on the wall of his house. Seeing that he was now supporting M'Intyre the mob threatened to pull this plaque down an act that he told that they could willingly do as he had not done this work to obtain any form of recognition but that they should also remember that none of them would have any immunity from the disease if the likes of the M'Intyre were not welcome.

Following up on this story, Timothy paid this highly respected man a visit and during the ensuing conversation found out that he to had read the New Testament.

Mr. Margary and Dr. Brown
Back in Chefoo Dr. Brown was building up a team of students carrying out translation and medical work. One

of his friends was a Mr. Margary of the consular service who regularly dined with Timothy and Mr. Lilley. Margary was later to meet a horrific death in western China when in 1895 he set out on a journey to Burma to escort a British mission back to China. Hearing rumours of discontent amongst the local population Margary went on ahead to reconnoitre. He had only gone a few miles when he was set upon and butchered in Manwynne, the very first town over the Chinese border. The rest of the mission managed to turn round and make their way back to Burma fending off the hostile locals as they went. It was widely assumed that the murder had been officially sanctioned and diplomatic negotiations immediately took place to defuse the situation. From these series of meetings the "Chefoo Convention" was agreed from which an apology was made to the British Government and four new ports were opened up to foreign trade,

With Brown, Timothy set out for a tour of healing and preaching. They travelled by boat since the canals in the region were numerous and it was by far the easiest mode of transport. The most common boat was obviously man powered and called the foot-boat as the boatman would steer or paddle with his hands and row with his feet. His whole life would be spent on board as he would cook and eat whilst travelling. Moving gate locks had not been invented then and the canals would accommodate the change of heights required by the use of a "pah". This was basically a dam with a gentle smooth sloping slide going from the higher level on one side of the dam down to the lower level on the other side. This slope was well greased with mud and when raising the boat a rope was attached and a number of men would winch it up using two wooden windlasses. Going down was a much more adventurous affair where the boat was driven to the top edge and eased over with one man balancing it from front to back until it would plunge down the slope restrained by a rope as it hit the lower level with a tremendous bow wave. Something similar is still employed at Oxford on the Isis, to allow punts to negotiate a weir but instead of a muddy slope metal rollers are used over which the flat-bottomed punts travel. When the canal ceased to allow them to travel in the direction that they desired they could transfer to a sedan – a chair with poles either side so that two men could carry them. These bearers would move at a slow rhythmic pace stopping frequently for a drink and smoke at one of the many tea shops along the way. Care had to be taken as to which side you alighted from as most bearers were highly superstitious, if you got out of wrong side they would immediately run away holding their hands to their heads and shouting that they would all be dead within a year. The only remedy for such a catastrophe was for them to walk on to the next shrine and burn incense sticks and then return to carry out their task. For longer journeys the use of mules, horses or camels was the norm. Variations of these modes of transport – you could be carried in a wheelbarrow by one man, or a sail assisted cart, when the ground was flat, and even the luxury of a non-sprung mule cart solidly built to withstand the worst of conditions but very efficient at throwing the occupants around in the most bruising way possible. The smoothest method was to be slung high on two mules, one behind the other; this was the way they invariably chose to travel.

This trip proved to be inspirational for both of them. Brown's medical knowledge and subsequent treatment of his patients won the confidence of those he came into contact with. The attendance to the clinic gradually grew in number as the supplies and the back up required to look after the mule trains became ever larger with a large contingent of volunteers willing to be a part of his miracle cures. Eventually they were taking over whole inns with the innkeepers generally refusing to accept any payment so that they were seen to be "good men".

In the winter of 1874 Timothy was again on his own as Dr. Brown was summoned back to New Zealand to take a post as professor in Dunedin University. At this time of year there was little or no movement of steamers along the coast north of Shanghai due to the coastal harbours and rivers being ice bound, this made it ideal for Timothy to increase his knowledge of the Chinese language and to attend and give lectures at the various clubs and societies formed by the foreign residents. One meeting proved to be very well attended, the subject being "Demonic Possession in China"

This meeting became very popular with members of all religions, believers and non-believers alike turning up at the discussions. In China demonic possession was quite prevalent – a product of religion, sects, social structure and simple beliefs. Remember, the persecution of witches had not long passed in Britain and there was still an underlying belief that they did indeed exist in certain isolated areas which required the need for exorcisms. The subjects at the meetings were varied and ranged from people being possessed – the most common examples being those who adopted the persona of someone who was dead, or in the spirit world, and these would talk in a strange voice or tongue. At the other extreme they would have residents who often claimed that their houses were haunted and who were too terrified to live in them. For this reason some properties had been vacant for over twenty years.

Many of those possessed by these so-called demons did convert to Christianity and their new found faith did give them the strength to overcome their problems and at the same time strengthen Timothy's mission. Exorcisms of haunted properties took place allowing the residents to return, refurbish them and live a new life. One ploy Timothy used was to have one of his fellow missionaries sleep overnight in such a place and then declare the following morning that he had had a very restful night. Such was the fear in one family that no sooner had one exorcism taken place in their house; the next door neighbours then complained that the ghost had moved into their property which in turn had to be exorcised.

At another meeting a Jewish man stated that demonic possession was brought to Palestine from Persia where it had obviously spread outwards to the East, another medically trained man discounted the fact of such a phenomenon saying that it was generally down to individual physical problems manifesting in different forms of hysteria. These meetings were obviously lively and informative.

Mrs Holmes

The Baptist missionaries did not necessarily enjoy a smooth life with their families. Adoption of local children was quite common and Mrs Holmes, the wife of an American Baptist missionary adopted two boys. One of these [Joe] on reaching sixteen ran away to Russia. To prevent the other doing the same thing she sent him to America. When he returned from his American schooling she got him a job in the British Consulate only to find out that he was using his position in the Customs Office to plot a rebellion against the Government and was allowing arms and munitions to be imported into the country. When he was discovered he immediately fled back to America where he then repaid the sacrifices made to educate him by turning his back on Christianity and promoting Confucianism. At the same time her maternal son became a medical practitioner but used his position to extract money from his patients.

When Mrs. Holmes fell ill her son did little for her so she returned to America, poor and in ill health, she wrote to Joe, who had now returned to China after earning good money in Russia. He immediately sent all of his savings to his adopted mother thanking her for giving him the chance of a new life.

Later Timothy was to be the recipient of Joe's generosity when he was moving from Tientsin to Shanghai. Joe now a successful businessman sent a team of men to clear Timothy's house and move all the contents on to the steamer he was to use. Nothing went missing and Joe refused any payment.

In 1874 Timothy again visited Chi-nan-Fu [*Jinan*] with a large entourage. The journey proved difficult, the heavy summer rains had created the usual quagmire. The carters were inevitably were forced to leave the impassable churned up roads and drive into the fields.

This consequently brought them into conflict with the farmers and Timothy many times had to use all his diplomatic skills to prevent any fights breaking out. It became clear to him that the reason why the roads were in such a bad state of repair was due to the fact that there was no form of governance or organisation that covered communications, certainly not nationally and definitely very limited on a local level.

Mr Li

In Chi-nan-Fu he was visited by another of his fellow missionaries and a Chinese medical assistant called Li. One of the problems they all faced when treating illnesses was catching the diseases themselves. Li succumbed to Typhoid and Timothy took it upon himself to nurse him back to health. For a month he would wake up on the hour every hour and feed Li a light chicken soup. Li kept haemorrhaging so badly that the outlook looked pretty grim, but in the third week he gradually improved and started to become his usual irritable self, demanding to be allowed to return to Chefoo. [*Yantai*] He was duly despatched in the comfort of a sedan chair.

Such generosity of spirit by giving no thought to his own danger helped Timothy win the confidence of the Chinese.

The causes of diseases around this time were not known and consequently exposure to causal factors continued. Cleanliness and good sanitation were not often possible and it was not known that the louse carried typhus, the mosquito malaria or yellow fever all of which would break out occasionally.

Li Hung Chan

Being based in Chefoo he came into contact with one of the most influential members of Chinese society – Li Hung Chan. He had become famous in China as one of the leading generals who had broken up the Taiping rebellion. General Gordon [of Kartoum fame] had actually served with him. He was a ruthless man causing Gordon at one time to seek him out with the intention of killing him since he had massacred a group of rebel generals that Gordon had somehow managed to persuade to surrender on the promise that he would protect them. Li was sent to negotiate the Chefoo" Convention" [see Mr. Margary]. To help with negotiations Li had travelled with a substantial retinue of servants and advisors. Timothy, when told by his Chinese assistant, heard that many of this retinue were suffering from dysentery and rheumatism. On hearing this he sent a parcel of quinine and chlorodyne, the medicines used at that time to alleviate such conditions, to General Li's headquarters. A letter of thanks was sent back.

Chefoo was fast becoming a resort for foreigners to recuperate as its climate was far more equitable than the hot and damp south. However, it was not in an area of influence within China although from the point of view of missionary work it was the centre of all the northern missions. Timothy wanted desperately to get into the heart of the country and to meet those who had not had, as he saw it, the benefit of western learning.

Following up on his research he found that certain sects resided in Ch'ing – chou – fu, some two hundred miles away, who had a large number of followers that were intent seeking a higher knowledge than that provided by the three main indigenous religions of China. He saw them as people who would be more sympathetic to the Christian teachings that he wanted to give. There were then many kinds of secret sects in China, many using initiation rites, passwords and meeting only in the most secure surroundings, usually at night-time. As most of these sects were subversive they were banned. Some have survived to this day, mostly through the use of fear and gangs to exert a strict discipline.

Needless to say Timothy would seek only those with higher ideals. He found some that opposed the worship of idols and others that found the main religions of China lacking.

He set out in the middle of the 1875 winter with the fourteen-year-old son of a sea captain. The weather grew progressively worse. The first day they only made ten miles, the second five. The snow turned to blizzard obliterating the road. They had to drive their horses across fields occasionally coming into conflict with villagers. With two days travel left to complete the journey they were hit by a major blizzard. Not being able to see where they were going, they were lucky enough to stumble across a wayside inn. There they met other travellers who were also sheltering. These men were not so lucky as some of the carters they had employed to carry their provisions had perished in the icy cold wasteland and they would now have to wait until the weather improved so that they could access their provisions and employ new helpers.

There was nothing to do but sit it out and wait.

6 – New Horizons

Eventually they arrived at Ch'ing-chou-fu having endured the most arduous conditions possible. The name of the city translated into the prefectural city [Fu] of the Green [Ching] District [Chou]. Its location was ideal as far as Timothy was concerned. The city was a Manchu garrison holding the largest number of troops south of Peking. Around the outside of its substantial walls ran a wide and very deep canal. Although he had arrived to an indifferent welcome, he managed eventually to find an inn that would put him up for a long period. The city was in a densely populated area some 250 miles from the nearest seaport [Chefoo] but on the edge of a highly fertile plain. It was in the middle of the Shantung province and had a backdrop of an imposing range of mountains some 1200 feet high. It was a walled city topped with large defensive crenulations. It was also a very ancient city built before Christian times and home to many important princes each with their own court. It had definitely seen better times, was somewhat run down but it was still imposing in the greatness and majesty of its old Imperial buildings that had once echoed to the wealth and pomp of Royal and civic ceremonies. The city itself was spacious, as most of the population lived in the surrounding districts, the need for their labour no longer required other than for growing crops and raising farm animals.

There were several smaller walled cities in the prefecture, which comprised eleven counties each with their centre of administration, and each surrounded by small towns and those in turn by smaller villages. Timothy made no attempt to find a house. Whilst he was in an inn he was a guest – if he procured or rented a house then he was deemed to be looking for permanent residence and this would have raised possible opposition. Whilst they were dressed in foreign clothing they were objects of curiosity and this brought many visitors to the inn, unfortunately mostly out of inquisitiveness. Timothy then realised that he would only be able to integrate with these country people, [they had never seen a European], by adopting the Chinese form of dress. When he did this the effect was immediate. He started to receive invitations to tea at various houses. It was during one of these visits that he was told that he had been held responsible for an outbreak of broken windowpanes in the city – this was not as bad as it seemed when he realised that the broken panes were not caused by any form of maliciousness, but by curiosity. Each window pane was made of thin rice paper and in order to see him people would wet their fingers to create a spy hole to watch him as he passed.

He had often wondered why there was no glass in China – no glass containers or bottles or window panes. The reason gradually dawned on him. Glass had been discovered in the Arabian desserts when the nomadic tribes lit fires at night to cook and keep themselves warm. The high silica content within the sand coupled with the heat caused the sand fuse into a semi transparent mass. The sands in China were of a different composition and so this accidental discovery never occurred. Coupled with fact that glass containers were never required since they had discovered many centuries previous how to make porcelain so fine and delicate to produce smooth cups from which they could drink tea.

It was 1875 and the Chinese Emperor had died. The whole country went into mourning and the worst affected were the barbers as all men had to remain unshaven during the mourning period. Timothy duly "mourned" with the rest.

His acceptance with the public grew ever stronger in the summer of that year when there was another outbreak of cholera. Using chlorodyne, a famous patent medicine sold in the British Isles. Dr. John Collis Browne, a doctor in the British Army in India, invented it in the 19th century; and advertised it widely, its principal ingredients being a mixture of laudanum (an alcoholic solution of opium), tincture of cannabis, and chloroform, it was excellent for relieving pain, as a sedative, and for the treatment of diarrhoea. Clearly not the same product now found in chemists for the treatment of coughs and colds! He also used spirits of camphor and successfully treated the wife of the Superintendent of Police. Placing a few drops on sugar and administrating it every five minutes the wife, who apparently was on the verge of dying. When she completely recovered it resulted in much rejoicing in her family and Timothy's fame spread even further, even into the upper echelons of Chinese society. In the autumn he was called to treat several cases of "ague" or malarial fever. His treatment being very effective caused his reputation to become further enhanced although he still refused to be called a doctor.

Word of his work in the community reached the prefectural Treasurer, another person of high authority. His problem was slightly different from the ones that he normally came across. He was fifty, had no son and was desperate to father an heir. Timothy realised that the most likely cause was his heavy opium smoking so he placed him on a strict regime to gradually wean him off his habit. He allowed him to visit his study as often as he liked in order to avoid the company of, and therefore the temptation of, his fellow opium smokers. The Treasurer would sit and smoke tobacco from a clay pipe over a metre in length. To light it he had to use an incense stick about half a metre long which took a lot of skill and patience. Although he was an intelligent man he was taken aback when Timothy suggested the simple expedient of reducing the length of the pipe to ease the problem of targeting the small bowl. This he did and from then on brought only small tapers which were of course cheaper and easier to obtain. Both of them gained from their daily meetings, the Treasurer being in awe of Timothy's knowledge of the world outside China. In return he invited Timothy to be his Master of Feng-shui and choose a grave site for him. Feng-shui was regarded as a science in China and had channelled the Chinese attitude to life for many centuries; many of those who were resident in China at this time thought it was one of reasons why the country was held back from modernisation and progress. As it was explained to him it is "the art of adapting the residence of the living and the dead to co-operate and harmonise with the local currents of the cosmic breath". The dual Yin-yang, supposed to flow in currents should have no interference. From this the forms of buildings mountain ranges and the course of water and roads all had to be considered.

Feng-shui had held back development in China to a considerable degree. The development of mines, the construction of railways and roads as did the setting up of telegraph poles and wires all had to go through the process of obtaining balance and direction associated with this "science" often ending up with a negative response.

Timothy went with the Treasurer to his family village. After having tea with him at his farm, which was near the proposed site, he picked out what he considered to be the best position, this was dutifully marked out with bricks. Whether it was ever used, or what thoughts the family had on the matter Timothy never found out.

The Treasurer did become a firm friend and was concerned that Timothy was constantly being interrupted at the inn by passing travellers and those that were just plain curious. He asked why he was not in a permanent residence of his own. The process of renting property in China was difficult enough – for a foreigner even more so. You had to find someone that would guarantee that you were honest and would be a good neighbour. They would also have to stand security for you. When Timothy explained that as a foreigner most people thought that he was bad, not only that but no one knew him. The Treasurer was incredulous that such a simple thing stood in his way and, after asking if that was all there was to it excused himself and left the subject standing. Next day there was a knock on the inn door and the treasurer led Timothy to a pretty whitewashed house and said he could move in immediately and that he would stand security for him. It was all that Timothy had dreamed of and within three days he had installed himself in a delightful apartment overlooking a courtyard that was carefully looked after by the landlord. It had many plants in pots around the edge and these were watered and tended daily. Timothy had three rooms in all around a central one which could and was used as a meeting room. To one side was a smaller room with a stone floor under which ran flues carrying the heat from the fires that were lit in them. In winter he made this his bedroom and study, the other two rooms had clay or mud floors and these were cooler in the hot summer months. Outside his bedroom window was an orchard of mulberry trees and the landlord used the leaves of to feed the silkworms, which obviously boosted his income. His rent was paid in Mexican dollars at the rate of four and a half every moon. [China had still not adopted the month as a measure of time]. He found his diet was much more varied as in the south rice was the staple diet and meat was in short supply and when available invariably consisted of either pork or chicken. In the north a greater variety of meat was on offer with pork and chicken being in plentiful supply plus the additional choice of lamb, mutton and on occasions beef. Having spent most of his time in inns he did not have the knowledge or facilities to cook and store his provisions. So he fell back to using the local native restaurant or bought cooked food from the local market. This was not really recommended as they could be the means of passing on whatever disease was rampant at the time, be it typhoid, dysentery or cholera. Nevertheless he got by without too much trouble.

He developed some interesting recipes. Breakfast would consist of a millet gruel that he would cover with a thick layer of raw brown sugar. The sugar acted as insulation and would keep the contents warm for at least an hour. He would eat this with a wafer thin millet pancake bought first thing in the morning. Even in these outlying country areas, he still managed to obtain "foreign" butter which he would liberally spread over the pancake. For lunch he would go out on the street and buy about four rice dumplings from a stall or vendor's barrow or from hawkers carrying them around in baskets on the end of poles carried across their shoulders. These dumplings would come wrapped in a large leaf. His evening meal was usually consumed in a restaurant with first course of soup normally *chi-p'ien* [a light chicken consommé] or *yil-pien* the same type of consommé but made from fish, with this he would have some small steamed loaves and finish off with a local tea. During winter he would start his meal with a hot yellow rice wine that soon spread warmth throughout his body.

He used this opportunity to converse with other diners and obtain the latest update on local news. There was a surprising variety of restaurants since the type of food and method of cooking differed considerably between the religions and tribes. For instance there were Mohammedan and Korean restaurants.

This idyll did not last for long for onto the scene came a retired mandarin, violently anti-foreign and intent on making life as difficult as possible for the landlord. He complained loudly especially in public about his association with and apparent welcoming of those that were living off the good nature of simple people. It became so intense that the landlord was forced to go to the Governor of the three prefectures that he ruled over, one of which was Ch'ing-chou-fu, to see if he could end the harassment. He came back with an order from the governor to show the mandarin that he had personally issued a proclamation earlier that peace had to be maintained between all foreigners and citizens and emphasised the fact that the Treasurer having stood as security should be enough authority. Not satisfied with that, the mandarin took his complaint to the City Magistrate to see if he could get the order overturned. The Magistrate was forcibly direct and told him in no uncertain manner that since there were many foreigners co-existing peacefully in Peking plus the fact that Timothy was giving away medicine and treating the sick and poor, he should be grateful and actually thank him and stop antagonising him. Needless this was taken with bad grace and he stored his smouldering resentment for almost a year before the opportunity arose for him to attack Timothy again.

Famine was a regular occurrence in all the various parts of China and in 1876, one happened in the area. To take up the children abandoned by their families, Timothy established an orphanage. Some of the parents were driven to suicide, often by such bizarre means such as chewing the heads of matches and dying a slow lingering death from phosphorus poisoning or swallowing gold leaf or lead. Jumping down wells or into the raging rapids on the rivers was common. One of Timothy helpers, a Chinese B.A. was taking an orphan to this refuge when the ex-mandarin, still carrying his enormous chip on his shoulder, suddenly appeared and accused him of procuring the child for use by foreigners. Giving him as good as he got Timothy's helper watched in disbelief as shouting loudly, the mandarin disappeared into the town claiming that he now had the evidence to get him removed.In order to nip this in the bud, Timothy sent a note to the Prefect stating that the old anti-foreign feelings were being stoked up by the usual person and if he wanted to he was welcome to visit him to see the work that was going on and satisfy himself that all was well. This the Prefect did and then sent out a proclamation stating that anyone who looked after orphans was a public benefactor and any person found circulating false reports either in writing or by word of mouth would be dealt with in the civil courts. This ensured not only the foundation and continuance of his mission but also guaranteed the on-going smouldering resentment of his adversary.

Now settled in and with many contacts and friends, Timothy began to study Chinese religion and the role that different sects played in this. Obtaining a copy of the *Ching Hsin Lu* or "Record of Devout Faith" he immersed himself in the collection of the most popular Confucian and Taoist tracts. He then went on to read two volumes of a handwritten copy of the Buddhist *Diamond Classic,* copying it himself to assist in memorising all of the passages. From this he wrote a catechism or book of questions and answers [this was a common method used at the time to improve an individuals intellectual capabilities] but looking at the Chinese religions from a Christian point of view. He made sure that he did not use "foreign" terms but substituted Chinese expressions thus giving access to those Chinese that could read them but not appearing to force opinions upon them. This time was well spent as he continued to translate other religious works into Chinese.

He was now well based to approach leaders of other religions in the area and since Gh'ing-chou was an important Mohammedan centre with its own theological college, several mosques of different sects and with even more of them located out in the countryside he decided to make a direct approach to the Moslem leaders.

Having requested a visit he was given a date when he could meet with the college professors, religious elders and principal mullahs. It must have been very intimidating for Timothy to enter the main hall where all were gathered, although able to communicate in Chinese he was not exactly fluent and certainly not up to the standard of the academics to whom he was now the centre of attention. The head of the college received him formally and after some refreshments he was placed in the seat of honour. Discussions then took place about different countries. They wanted to know how much knowledge he had of Arabia and Egypt. They plied him with questions about Europe and asked him to describe his journey around the Horn of Africa and then on to China. He was then treated to a carefully prepared address by the host in which he described the founding of Moslem faith and how Jesus was seen from their perspective. At the end of this Timothy thanked his host for an illuminating address and for his kindness and courtesy and promised that he would return for further talks on another day.

On his return home he felt that this visit had been a turning point. Here he was faced with a rival creed with all the claims of infallibility that were also claimed in his own religion. He realised that for every prophecy that he could quote, for every miracle he could produce they could counter with many more. It was a salient moment for reflection.

To be able to argue from a point of strength he was now driven to study the Islamic faith, to develop his own opinions and not to be guided by preconceived Christian ideas or ideological tracts handed down through the generations – in other words he would question everything and would hopefully arrive at what he could consider the truth.

It was not long before he had another invitation to attend the college and when he arrived he found that the Moslem Principal had surrounded himself with about twelve of his students and again he was given another sermon. On completion of this Timothy thanked him and asked if he could reply to the points made. Having found that the students reacted positively to Timothy's comments it transpired that the leaders had later decided that future meetings would always be without the students in attendance, presumably to avoid them being exposed to anything that might undermine their faith. In this he abjectly failed to establish any further discourse with the Moslem faithfull although one old mullah did continue to visit him. This learned man quoted various Persian and Arabian authorities to prove his points. Timothy stopped him and said that his arguments were based on the knowledge of men who were great in their day but the world had moved on. He [Timothy] had travelled through countries that they never knew existed and was well versed in their differing customs and religious beliefs. The mullah countered that they had all written under the guidance of the spirit of God and therefore could not be wrong. Timothy's reply was that he too wrote under the Spirit of God and would not have been in China today but for this. The mullah thought long and hard, rose, and said to Timothy that he was sad that he had not had the wisdom to listen more intently to a messenger from God and that he was now a wiser and more humble man.

This meeting of minds was all the more remarkable when considering that only a few years earlier there had been a Moslem uprising in western China which had only finally been put down some months earlier after the wholesale destruction of cities, towns and villages and the slaughter of millions of Moslems. This reaction should be seen against the normal relations that the Chinese rulers had with the various religions, which were amicable providing they did not stray into each others political territory. It was this political agitation by the Moslems at the time that resulted in such a backlash. Needless to say it took a lot of persuasion from Christian based missions that they too were not politically motivated. Sometimes authorities in certain areas were not convinced of these arguments with the resultant feeling from earlier missionaries that they were sitting on a powder keg expecting the fuse to be lit at anytime.

This was made even clearer to him when he accepted an invitation by one of the heads of a minor sect to visit him in his mountain retreat. Timothy decided to do the journey on foot in spite of the fact that it was July and very hot. Before he could see the headman, one of his henchmen made it abundantly clear to Timothy that he was not welcome and made sure his reception was as hostile as it could be made. His attitude to Timothy and indeed to all westerners had been coloured by some publications he had seen with illustrations on surgical techniques. This he had assumed was the Christian manual for carving up the dead and was typical of their inhumanity to others. Timothy exhausted from his journey felt unable to respond and after a short rest told his host that he had travelled to see him with best of intentions but realised that after his reception it was probably a mistake. The headman told him to rest further as the man concerned would be leaving soon. The next day the two of them had a long and deep philosophical discussion, which helped to bond them. When the time came for Timothy's departure one of the headman's servants was instructed to guide him over the mountains so that he could visit others who could benefit from his knowledge.

The time came when the guide had to leave Timothy and after bidding farewell Timothy decided to rest from the heat under the shade of a tree. Several labourers passed on by as he sat there each giving a cursory greeting but one came over and asked where he was heading for. On hearing Timothy's plans he told him that the next river was impassable but he would be welcome to stay in the next village until the waters had subsided. Thus he found himself in the local schoolmaster's house where he was given dinner and sat and conversed with the family when a group of villagers came in offering to help him across the river. When he got there it turned out to be over a hundred yards wide, and in full spate. With no bridge to cross and this being the only ford for many miles the villagers formed a ring around him and with water at chest height helped him across. He was nearly swept off his feet more than once but the locals held on to each other and knowing the best route guided him across. He was at a loss as to how to thank them when one of the group said that when they had visited Ch'ing –chou a long time back he had welcomed them, given them tea, answered all their questions and this was the least they could do to repay his courtesy.

He then found out that there was someone who he had met previously living in the next village. When he arrived he was given another warm welcome and was introduced to an elderly scholar who had about half a dozen students preparing for a degree in the local university. He was invited to have a meal with the teacher and his students who were intent on absorbing as much of the information he gave out as possible. This carried on after they had finished eating and each of them gave him a fan to sign. This was the equivalent of the modern autograph book since these signed fans were always displayed with pride in their homes especially those of notable or well known persons. What Timothy did was to write a verse of an English hymn on one side and make them promise to translate it into their own language on the other side.

His next stop was at another town where there was an innkeeper who had visited him frequently in the past. Again he had another grand welcome and this time he found himself amongst a group of Taoists who were holding a religious gathering. What was different was that all the delegates were women. It was down to the women in their communities to pray for good harvests the birth of a son etc. He was soon an object of curiosity with delegate after delegate coming to see the strange looking visitor. The questions that were asked revolved around foreign farming methods, parenting and western religion – an ideal opportunity for him to explain the reason for his presence.

Out of courtesy he called on the head Taoist priest and was invited to witness their great midnight ceremony. During the day the women brought their offerings, such as millet or other produce. These donations were then listed opposite their names on a long sheet of yellow paper and duplicated. One of these lists was then pinned up on a board in the temple and the other kept so that it could be burned before the main divinity of that temple. The idea behind this was that as they burned and the pieces of paper floated into the air so would the names of the donors' head towards their god. This always took place at midnight and the temple would be filled with women, the priest would burn incense, repeat incantations and then set fire to list of names.

Timothy returned home feeling much more hopeful. He had gained a small network of acquaintances from previous meetings and acts of charity or kindness, and he had now met many more and developed a mutual respect amongst those he had met in the villages and towns he had visited. In general he had been welcomed warmly, in a few cases he had met aggression and antagonism but he was still all too aware that as a stranger and a foreigner he was exposed, isolated and vulnerable.

Having been submitted to the teachings of Buddhism and Taoism Timothy took a radical step for the time. Both religions had abundant literature that that were tailored to suit the educated and simpler versions for uneducated. Buddhism especially used a philosophy to test the powers of the greatest Chinese scholars whilst still catering for those with limited education. Up to this time successive missionaries had not considered adapting any of this for their own needs. What he did was to virtually censor these native tracts and rewrite them removing all clauses that were not consistent with his Christian beliefs. He also drew up a catechism of the Christian religion. He gave this to a silk weaver who had declared his desire to become a Christian who then committed it to memory. This did not go as smoothly as he had expected as the weavers wife became quite distraught, as she was convinced that her husband would be going to heaven leaving her behind. To get over this the husband taught her and his two children all he knew with the net result being that they both asked to be baptised. This was unique and was a breakthrough for Timothy as the act of immersion in water was unknown in China. However he had to be careful in case the process was misunderstood, not by the two concerned, but by friends, neighbours or observers of the act but also because a woman was involved. He decided to conduct the Baptism outside the West Gate of the city where a beautiful clear river swept in a curve around a nearby Buddhist temple. In order not ruffle any feathers he exercised his growing diplomatic skill by calling on a Buddhist monk that he had befriended some time earlier and having explained the process asked if he could use a couple of rooms in the temple as changing rooms. The monk readily gave his consent and watched as the ceremony took place.

Over the following months he succeeded in baptising a further fifteen people, more than any other pioneer missionary. These were carried out in the courtyard of his home and to ensure that no false reports emanated from what was going on, he made sure that his friend, the Treasurer was present to witness each one.

*Newspaper image of Timothy
carrying out famine relief*

7 – Famine

Nothing can be more distressing or give the feeling of utter helplessness than to witness famine. In China, with its vast burdening population and marginal resources [it may have a large landmass, but 90% of it is incapable of supporting food production the remainder being mostly desert or mountain] One of the greatest famines in China occurred over a three year period during 1876 to 1878. China had frequent periods of food shortage due primarily in the south to floods and high rainfall and in the north to drought. These three years were rainless and as a consequence the area around Shansi over a radius of a thousand Li [length] which was the equivalent of five hundred miles contained thousands of dying or starving people many were driven by desperation to carrying out acts that were so horrific that many would have thought unthinkable.

In the first year the governing bodies and leaders of the various deities declared a fast banning the eating of meat especially beef. This was the easiest route to take as it combined necessity with religious edicts and made the implementation easier. Officials and crowds of people would gather at the different temples. On one occasion a Magistrate bound in chains followed by a large crowd walked to the Chief Temple and prostrated himself before the image as did the crowds behind him. Timothy took the opportunity during this initial period to ride from town to town to place placards on all the main entrances of the city gates imploring the populace to turn to God and not worship idols. Whether he thought that this would have any effect is not known as in such circumstances everyone was praying for rain in any case.

One hot day as he was resting in an inn after putting up one of his proclamations a deputation of elderly men came to him begging him to teach them how to pray to his god so that their families could be released from starvation. The drought was continuing with incessant stifling heat, the sun continually beating down and with it the price of food increased day after day. People started to become desperate. Robbery was on the increase; a boy of twelve was arrested for stabbing a man in an attempt to steal his food. A group of women raided a wealthy man's house, seized sufficient millet for a meal, cooked it, ate it and then marched on to another. The men, seeing the success of this enterprise, organised a band of vigilantes, about five hundred in all, who then went from village to village pillaging. As a result of this the Governor of Shantung stripped the Prefect and Magistrate of their badges of office and threatened to have them dismissed. He immediately ordered that all offenders were to be captured and beheaded. The leaders were to be held in the "sorrow cage", a metal construction in which they could neither stand nor sit and there they stayed in agony until they died of starvation. Each day executions were held just behind Timothy's courtyard until order was finally restored.

Those that had any grain left over from the previous year guarded it as if it were gold dust; those that were poorer and had no grain could only expect to go another year enduring the agony of hunger pains. One June day when visiting a small village he sat in an inn and ordered some cakes for his lunch. As he looked out the window he could see a group of thin malnourished children sitting in the shade under a tree with baskets full of thistles and various green leaves. As they sat chewing these he called them over and asked if they were willing to do an exchange. He would give them some of his cakes if they would give him a few green leaves. The boys were ecstatic, they had not tasted any flour based food for months, so much so that one of them had a terribly swollen face from chewing excessive amounts of the "Huai" tree [*Sophora Japonica*] to which it was obvious that he had had an allergic reaction.

The next move came when the Governor removed all taxes on the import of grain and increased the purchase of grain from Kiangsu and Manchuria and then sold it at less than cost price. Unrest was growing rapidly. Elected heads were being urged by the villagers to lead them into rebellion against the government. One man refused to join in this and fled, with his family to Ch'ing –chou where they were all killed when the pursuing villagers caught up with them..

Near to his house Timothy, for the first time, witnessed the harrowing sight of mothers offering to sell their babies. Little did he know that this would presage even worse events in a very short time. A stream of what appeared to be highly educated men visited him asking if it were possible to become his disciples. What he had not realised was that they were in fact a deputation sent by other powerful people with one mission in mind, to persuade him to lead a revolution for the starving people against the government. He had no choice but to tell them that it was not possible, any revolt would ultimately lead to further bloodshed and place him in an invidious position. Two days later another man from another town came and declared that the people in that area had met and that they were ready to rise up providing he would lead them.

This placed him in a very difficult position. Clearly, if the authorities got wind that he was involved in any form of insurrection, he would be tried and more than likely executed. He had to make sure that no rumours were flying around that may raise the suspicion of the authorities that he was involved in any plot. He had to do something and do it quickly. He had no means of buying grain or distributing it, his only recourse for providing relief was money, but he had only a little money of his own which could be supplemented by donations from friends in Chefoo., but distribution of this was fraught with danger. What if stories of this foreigner's wealth and generosity became widespread? He would be faced with teeming crowds around him begging for a share of whatever he had to offer, hunger could turn them into a dangerous mob. One Chinese threw cash from the city wall to the starving. The resultant mayhem left many dead. Another grain dealer decided to release his stock. The result was the same.

To overcome this, an edict was made by the local magistrate that no public distribution was to be made by anyone other than those acting under and for the local authorities.

Seeing the despair of those wandering the streets, Timothy devised a plan for the orderly issue of cash. He would choose a narrow lane so that everyone could only stand in a line. As he gave each one his handout, he would stamp the palm of their hand with aniline ink. Some, in an attempt to get more would go home and scrub it off so that when they presented a clean hand at the end of the queue they were soon sent packing.

To get over the problem of the constant stream of deputations asking him to lead a revolt, he resorted to telling each representative that he would have to report back to the Governor of the province. This appeared to curtail this form of pressure. His next problem came when he heard that groups of women were comparing his acts of kindness with the apparent indifference of the mandarins. Alarmed that if such reports were to get back to the officials they would react with hostility and he could end up in prison, he had no choice but to leave immediately, giving his landlord three months rent in advance. In his haste he failed to notice that he had a stowaway on his cart, a young boy intent on visiting his uncle in the provincial capital. This now compounded the issue, the boy's parents would be distressed, rumours of kidnapping would abound, as luck would have it he was fortunate that when asking the locals he managed to find someone who he could pay to deliver the boy safely back home. When he returned later his worst thoughts were confirmed. The kidnapping rumours were all around. To clear his name he persuaded the boy's father to accompany him to the local seat of government where the father publicly proclaimed his gratitude to the foreigner and his kindness in making sure that his son returned home, this closed the matter and no further mutterings were heard.

Moving on to Chi-nan-fu he managed to obtain an interview with the Governor, a man of great personal presence who had been one of the principal antagonists of the Tai-ping rebels. He had successfully prevented them expanding northwards after they had overrun thirteen of the eighteen provinces in the south. Timothy sat with him and ran over his vision as to how they might fight famine by developing the vast mineral deposits that were currently only being scraped from the surface of the province. China, he told him, had a vast mineral wealth that the rest of the world needed to feed its rapidly growing industries. He proposed the introduction of railways to transport this resource to the ports, the construction of which would provide much needed work for the peasant population and with the ongoing mining and support facilities, long term employment and stability.

Here we were in 1876 without a single line having been laid, primarily due to opposition from religious leaders, and the first attempts were about to be made to lay a line from Shanghai over the twelve miles to Woosung. This was actually completed within a year but the same old fears were raised – it would disturb the spiritual powers. This led to the Chinese Government taking it over from private hands and dumping the rolling stock on a beach in Formosa [Taiwan] where it rotted away. In 1877 an English engineer was given permission to build an eleven-kilometre railway to transport coal from the Tong-shan mine to a new deep-water port. His remit was that it had to be a horse-powered railway which, being an engineer, he interpreted in engineering terms and built the Chinese equivalent of the "Rocket". This one off machine was never used and ended up on display in a museum.

He managed to fire up the interest of the Governor only to be foiled in furthering his vision by the Governors promotion to Viceroy of the Ssu-ch'tian province. All was not lost though as the Governors son later became a friend of his in Shansi.

Returning to Ch'ing –chou he started to get concerned about the number of followers he was attracting especially those who were driven to expect miracles to end their incessant hunger. Crowd control became a matter of priority as he watched the swaying masses before him. It was then that he had another flash of inspiration and insisted before he gave any talks or sermons that the crowd had to sit. In a stroke he solved the problem of crushing and the potential of panic. This he did at his first meeting in a large threshing house opposite his house. He sat the expectant crowd in rows and told them quite frankly that he did not have much money but that he would dole out all of it by giving a little amount to every person present. If there was some left over he would repeat the task again and again until it all ran out. All of this was conducted in complete silence and the mandarins present were astonished at this example of crowd control. After issuing all of monies he told all present that if the rain didn't come even the government could not save them and then asking them to kneel he prayed that their suffering would be over.

This form of relief was about to be stopped as the Magistrate had decided to issue a proclamation against the distribution of private charity, so on receipt of his shipment of money from Chefoo Timothy felt obliged to hand it over to the Magistrate for him to distribute accordingly. This went down very well and pleased the authorities; they were able to purchase what little grain there was in area, albeit at a greatly inflated price due to its scarcity. Another consequence of drought meant that land had little value and now failed to find buyers even at a third of its previous asking price; furthermore furniture and clothing had virtually no value at all.

Timothy's unflagging interest in the well being of the ordinary people held him in good stead. So much so that a sufficient number of people were interested enough to consider forming a small church. To these he gave translations of the bible and simple books on Christianity, which most memorised. The number soon swelled to sixty, all of whom having read and memorised the scriptures considered themselves to be leaders who in turn could spread their thoughts amongst their fellows. Timothy supplied them with empty rooms to which they would bring their own bedding and food. He even supplied separate facilities for gatherings of female leaders. All of these then established adult Sunday schools where they worshipped together, within a year he had over a thousand members interested in furthering their knowledge on Christian teachings. Others adopted Timothy's approach but their numbers invariably declined when the pivotal organiser moved on. Timothy was determined to stay or at least remain in contact with his flock and consequently did not expand his area of influence too quickly or too far.

Further contributions towards famine relief now started to reach him from the foreign communities in Chefoo. To ensure orderly distribution he talked with his friend the Magistrate and together they decided to distribute this money in the isolated villages that were often overlooked. In order to establish some form of priority they sent out messengers to find out which communities were in most need.

When he arrived at the first town on this list, he found that there were three times the anticipated numbers of people requiring assistance. They had already eaten their mules, donkeys, cows and even their pets. The crowd soon became unmanageable and agitated. All of those who were local had been issued with tickets and in the melee there was no way that only those with tickets would make it to the front. Sizing up the situation, he left his assistants instructing them to start doling out the money as soon as the crowd had reached manageable proportions. He slowly but obtrusively started to move himself away from the crowd taking with him, as he had guessed, to a neighbouring hill those that did not have tickets. When he stopped, these unfortunates threw themselves to the ground pleading for help. Timothy, with the help of a local woman, told them a parable and explained that whilst today might not be their day, if they had faith, ultimately they too would be rewarded. The crowd then dispersed quietly and when he returned he found that the distribution had taken place peacefully. As the flow of funds increased, he was able to move from community to community thereby confirming his promise made to assist all in the locality.

He now moved on to establishing orphanages to look after the many children who had lost their parents through malnutrition and disease or who had simply been abandoned, as there was not enough food to feed them. His funding allowed him to set up five of these, each with five hundred orphans. These orphanages were invariably located in empty houses – so called haunted houses. To disprove that they were in fact haunted he would spend the first few nights in them. Invariably his assistants would disappear after the first night, scared off by all of the strange noises they heard. Timothy would remain alone listening to the rats and mice, which were the only evidence of evil spirits. One by one the assistants would return until all had plucked up enough courage to move in.

He now had the problem of what to do with five hundred boys and a limited amount of help. To overcome this particular problem he turned them into industrial training colleges and had supplies of tools sent in from China and abroad. Calling in local skilled workmen he was soon turning out employable young men capable of earning a livelihood. The next exposure to danger was on a journey to Ch'ang – lo. In order to carry out his relief work he had to carry a great deal of bullion. When he started out he would invariably go with some gold ingots. As he got near to his destination he would exchange these for a greater number of silver ingots. To enable a meaningful distribution to the local population this would in turn be changed into copper "cash" Thus he found himself in charge of three large carts full of cash at Wei-hsien. Finding that he was pressed for time he made the mistake of not informing the Magistrate at Cha'ng-lo of his imminent arrival and that the purpose of his journey was to distribute aid around and beyond the city. The Magistrate now took exception at what appeared to be an insult to his position. He ordered his men to block Timothy inside the inn's yard. Being unable to move his carts Timothy rode on horseback to the first village he was due to visit. There he found a large crowd of over a thousand had gathered all expectant. He dare not tell them of the position back at his base, as there would have been a mass riot and bloodshed if the starving, agitated crowd moved on to the city. To play for time he told the crowd that the aid had been delayed and asked that they appoint a leader from each village to take responsibility for collection and distribution and for all of the rest of them to depart. He then rode back to the city only to find that another crowd had gathered and were throwing stones at his assistant who was desperately trying to protect the carts and their precious cargo. He gave a short speech in an attempt to mollify the crowd, instructed his assistant to protect the carts for a further twenty minutes, and if he had not returned to grab five strings of cash and make his escape to a village some two miles away. Timothy then went to the Magistrates headquarters and barged his way to his office announcing that in a few minutes there would be no one in charge of the money and if there was any consequential rioting and deaths then it was on his head – he would have to bear the consequences. Turning his back on the Magistrate he left to go swiftly making sure his assistant was safe. The Magistrate, sizing up the situation, sent in more men to seize and protect the cash.

Making good his escape Timothy met up with his assistant and they hotfooted it to the next village. Exhausted, they were soon overtaken by a group of about six men who forcefully demanded that they return to the city to distribute their aid. The only way to extricate themselves from this confrontation was to hand over the whole of the five thousand cash that they had and tell them to give it to their villagers. Relieved at the mobs departure, they sat down to have a much-needed meal and had hardly started when another band of men armed with clubs and pitchforks burst in. These he recognised as villagers from an area where he had previously distributed aid. They, having heard he was in trouble, had formed a band to try and protect him and they insisted that he accompany them back to their village where he would be able to rest and feed in peace.

Reporting back to the Prefect at Ch'ing-chou Timothy agreed to get a receipt from the local Magistrate for the money that he had been authorised to distribute amongst the needy. As usual there was a delay on the part of the Magistrate and in no time at all another demonstration had been organised in the main square by over a hundred women each armed with a chopper and board. They all sat down and refused to move until the Magistrate came and explained why he was depriving the starving of their only means to buy food. When he eventually did show himself, he was greeted by chanting followed by the sound of over a hundred metal choppers crashing onto the boards. The effect was stunning, immediately he promised that distribution would commence the very next day.

Desperation was evident everywhere. People were pulling down their houses and trying to sell the wood; they were also dismantling the thatch and boiling it to provide some form of sustenance. As winter approached they dug great holes in the ground so that they could huddle together to provide warmth. They even resorted to leaving bodies on the ground to act as bait for the wolves and then attempt to trap the wolves for their meat. Women marched long distances outside the famine area and pleaded to be given to new owners as slaves.

With all this desperation and turmoil around him, Timothy decided to form the "Famine Relief" organisation in China. He had already established his credentials and was then able to open up the sources for the gifting of money, not only from the British but also from other countries, not only from Christian sources but also from other secular organisations and importantly, directly from the Chinese government itself. Most importantly was the trust he had built up with the Ch'ing-chou banking fraternity. He instigated a process to ensure that there was no overlapping or duplication of donations. This made a significant impression on those in government.

He had some even better news of help in November of 1876 when he was told that an old friend, Mr. A.G. Jones would be joining him in Chefoo. Timothy went there to ensure that Jones had settled in and then made the twelve-day journey back through snowdrifts to his headquarters. Jones was to join him four months later to assist with the famine relief scheme.

The first opportunity to change things came with the appearance of the spring crops. Timothy was determined that some of the modern western practices should be adopted to increase the crop yields. Treading another delicate path of change being thrust upon them by a foreigner he argued that all the elders and old sage kings of the country, who most of the population revered, had only attained their position by leading with the introduction of new ideas. However, this line of argument was not too well received by the majority as most were fearful of change, a point that was blatantly brought home when those that did advocate such ideas were lucky to escape with their lives when the Empress Dowager came onto the throne and instigated the anti-reform persecutions in 1898.

Meanwhile his congregation was growing apace. At this time the Old Testament had not been translated into Mandarin. There were few books on Christian teachings available to the ordinary reader and in consequence Timothy's writings were seized upon with great keenness as they were using his works as a means to teach themselves to read. One section of the populace in particular benefited from this. These were women, generally, over sixty, who had never received nor did they expect any form of education. Now they had the tools to hand and Timothy had an unexpected benefit in a new army to communicate his teachings. The number of churches under his supervision grew rapidly and in order to administer them he appointed unpaid agents, all of whom had been baptised, thus ensuring that his work was carried out in the most cost effective manner.

So he had now spent seven years in Shantung and his name "Li T'I-mo-t'ai was now spreading throughout the offices of influence in provinces from the high Mandarins down to the poorest and most humble.

TS'EN CH'UN HSUAN

Governor of Shansi and Timothy's friend and ally

8 – SHANSI – The months of desperation

Shantung had many advantages with regards to famine relief. Its long coastline meant that communication was relatively easy and relief supplies could be shipped nearer to the inland areas where help was needed. Shansi [Shanxi] was altogether different. To transport food to this North Western province by mule or horse was not logistically feasible, – the animal would consume more than the load it carried during the journey.

Shansi in 1877 had been hit by two years of very little rain – in some parts none had fallen at all. It was now evident that the rain was not likely to appear for a third year. Shansi was unique in several ways. It largely consisted of a great plateau mostly over two thousand feet in altitude. This plateau was covered in a rich fertile soil that only required a minimum amount of rain to produce bountiful crops but when dry virtually nothing germinated or grew. When news reached Shanghai of the dreadful conditions facing the population a Famine Relief Committee was formed and on hearing of Timothy's success in Shantung he was immediately requested to head up a similar organisation in Shansi. He discussed this request with his colleagues who urged him to go, they could carry on his good work and hopefully, be able to provide and organise any support he might require in his new challenge. There was no shortage of volunteers willing to accompany him on this mission of mercy.

Eventually he departed in the Arctic cold of a windswept November with one Christian farmer, his own servant and carrying a passport issued by the Viceroy of the Metropolitan Province. They travelled by mule drawn cart until they reached the mountains of Shansi on top of which lay the plateau. The mountain tracks were no longer capable of supporting the carts, so they left them behind and procured more mules on which they trekked up the narrow tracks, stopping for meals and overnight stays in inns that were cut into the soft stone of the cliffs. These hostelries were surprisingly warm as the cliffs structure comprised compacted fine loess which proved to be a good insulator.

The sights that greeted them as they made their way to the provincial capital, that once great city Tai-yuan-fu [Taiyuan] were truly horrific. The stench was awful with the bodies of those who had lain down by the roadside to die having already been torn apart by wolves and dogs. Some people had been subjected to this whilst they were still alive – too weak to defend themselves. Some of the dogs had been deliberately set loose to devour the bodies so that they could be recaptured and then killed for their meat. This "cannibalism by proxy" made it more acceptable to the starving. His two Chinese companions became so distressed that Timothy felt obliged to release them to return home. This they fully accepted leaving to him to continue on alone. When they eventually got back to Shantung and told their story to their compatriots they were made to feel so ashamed about leaving him to fend for himself that they felt obliged to return and eventually joined up with him again some weeks afterwards.

Timothy's first act was to call on the Governor, who happened to be the brother of the first Chinese minister to Great Britain. To say he was not pleased to have a foreign guest visit would be a gross understatement and every possible barrier was put in his way to make life difficult. Previously, this Governor had made a recommendation to the central government that one way of reducing "foreign" influence would be to play the Catholics off against the Protestants, so when Timothy did eventually get an audience with him and asked how best to use and distribute the relief funds he had at his disposal, the canny Governor told him that the Roman Catholic missionaries had approached him the week before for some grain for their orphanage so maybe he should hand his funds over to the them to enable the purchase of such items.

Carrying out his basic belief that the only way gain respect from authority was to carry out their wishes, he duly carried out the Governor's orders, meeting the Bishop and agreeing on the method of distribution. The only caveat Timothy put on the transaction was that he should have one of his own men present at the point of distribution in order to report back on the success or otherwise of the exercise. Unfortunately the Bishop refused to go along with this so Timothy wrote a report on the meeting and sent it to the Governor asking for his advice as to how it could be resolved this cleverly put the onus back on the Governor, where it really belonged. Such machinations always took some time to be digested so he decided that he would not waste valuable time and that he would visit the southern part of the province to see first hand the area under the greatest stress from starvation.

Before setting out he had managed to get the Bishop to agree to send out a questionnaire to the local priests in each district. From this he was able to asses the price that had been paid for grain before the famine, the current price, the number of new people who had moved into the area how many had died, how many cattle still remained uneaten and the number of women still left.

He set out on 28th January 1878 with only his manservant as company. This was highly risky as many of the starving were now turning to murder and cannibalism was rife, a foreigner would be a more likely and less conscience driven target. Each day they passed the dead and dying by the roadside – some naked – some well dressed. Starvation certainly did not respect class. Again, dogs, crows and magpies were devouring some the corpses. Ironically it was now that he saw that pheasants, rabbits, foxes and wolves were getting fatter as most of the humans had lost the will or strength to chase and kill them for food. Remarkably there was an absence of robbery in the towns and villages, as local courts would execute summary law on any offenders. As he approached one city gate he was greeted by a heap of naked male bodies piled one on top of the other – the stench of rotting flesh filled the air. On the other side of the gate was a similar pile, this time of women. All were naked, their clothes having been taken off and pawned for food. He found people baking cakes of clay impregnated with grass seed, twigs and any plant roots that could be found. A diet that was both insufficient and dangerous, in turn causing many more deaths. He noticed that all of the trees along the route were white where the bark had been ripped off to be cooked or eaten raw. Very few houses had doors or windows, the wood and paper having been sold for food or used as fuel. He saw cart after cart of women being taken away for sale so that their lives could be saved and any money gained providing food for the rest of the family. Everyone went armed with spears or swords or knives. Men would not go to the open coal pits to get much needed material to cook with and keep warm as they were almost certain to be ambushed, besides the mule owners and their animals had long since disappeared probably to the same fate. He now found that the scale of suffering prevented him from giving any relief and if he had tried he would have been surrounded by a starving mob. He decided that his only route was to return, report the facts and to organise on a sufficient scale a relief force that could stand some chance of making an impact.

Back in Tai-yuan-fu he set about trying to establish what could be done.

He found that the nearest stock of grain was at Tientsin, some 800 miles away accessed by poor roads and having to go over high altitude mountains invariably frozen and blasted by blizzards. The government itself, mindful of the predicament of the people facing starvation was trying to move these supplies but the great distances involved and steady drip of corruption at each stage of the journey and at each level of governance hampered any meaningful benefit to by the time it got to those affected. The logistical nightmare was compounded by the fact that the high mountain roads had been worn through the soft rock some ten, twenty feet below the level of the land meaning that only single file traffic was possible. These "channels" gradually filled up with mud and water and were becoming virtually impassable. This year was exceptionally cold. The yellow river had frozen over for the first time in over thirty years. Timothy on his journey back had taken the opportunity to measure and draw a map showing the elevation of this route. The plan, in the back of his mind, was to allow carts to travel by day and the slower camels by night. He also realised that the frozen river gave him the opportunity to use it as a level roadway. He had established from the returns of his questionnaire that proportionally, up to twenty million people must have perished in nine of the eighteen provinces of China.

Fortuitously, another missionary, the Rev. Arnold Foster who had also witnessed the conditions had to return to London due to ill health but was intent on raising the profile of what he had seen and to arouse public awareness. Just as he arrived at the office of the British minister to China – Sir Thomas Wade, so did Timothy's journal and letter. This had an immediate effect with a fund raising campaign, set up and was in full swing in next to no time.

Back in China, Timothy's next move was to set up an official authority for the distribution of the funds he was due to receive. This time his appeal; to the Governor was much more effective and an agreed number of villages were allotted to Timothy in which he could distribute his relief. Local officials and gentry were put at his disposal and under his direction set up, in the main towns and cities "soup kitchens" where millet gruel was given away. In one town 20,000 daily pots of gruel were being issued and in the villages 100 cash per head per month were distributed.

With the Governor firmly on his side Timothy was able to set up the distribution network very quickly. The Governor making sure that no corruption would be tolerated by executing an official who had siphoned off some of the funds. Timothy pleaded with the Governor to construct a railway to improve communications and the distribution of goods and services, the starving could be employed and paid for their work The Governor set up an enquiry but his officials came to the conclusion that this was a foreign idea and too many foreigners would have to be employed to oversee its construction and this in itself would be a constant source of trouble and provocation.

During this time Timothy was busy trying to ensure that any dignitary from China visiting England was shown all that was good in engineering, education and religion rather than spend their time at garden parties, theatres and visiting munitions and weapon factories etc. He also attempted to co-ordinate all the Protestant Missions in China in an attempt to reduce their waste and inefficiency by not competing with each other.

March 1878 saw the first steamer breaking through the ice and with it came a further group of missionaries David Hill of the Wesleyan Mission, Albert Whiting of the American Presbyterian Mission and Joshua Turner of the Chinese Inland Mission – all men of high influence. The famine had spread across the whole of the Northern provinces and with it disease on a scale not seen before.

Whiting died within a few days of his arrival, Turner was to devote the rest of his life to relief work around Tai-yuan-fu and Hill, a man of considerable wealth, from then on decided to lead a life of poverty devoting it through the time he was to remain in China to helping the poor. Timothy led the way forward and with Hill stood up to those that opposed their views – their work was eventually to establish the bedrock of Christianity around Shansi. [Shanxi]

As word got back to England about the tremendous work that was going on in China so did the amount of aid to assist the poor find its way east. Timothy, himself was now convinced that the only way to improve the lot of the ordinary Chinese was through education. As a friend of the poor both Timothy and David Hill had broken down the barriers of officialdom and had become friends of the gentry. But how to approach "Education"? Timothy was aware that thrusting Christian teachings at a suspicious audience was no way to gain converts or improve their lot. He had a great deal of sympathy for the Buddhists who were open to fresh teachings and had a yearning for enlightenment. With the increasing flow of funds strengthened by appeals from the Archbishop of Canterbury and the opening of a Mansion House Relief Fund by the Lord Mayor of London, Timothy had managed to arrange and organise the transportation of money together with the help of the Chinese Viceroy and an escort of soldiers to Tientsin. With the support of the Governor they then decided to move their operation closer to the centre of the famine and so set themselves up at P'ing-yang-fu. Help did come in a more indirect way

– for years officials and people had prayed to every god known to be associated with providing rain. An official had been told that in a certain well in the province there was an iron tablet possessing magical properties and maybe this would provide the solution. It was duly retrieved so that it could be used in prayers for rain. At the same time Catholics and Protestants were also praying for a downpour. When it did eventually come it flooded the whole province. With this all parties were happy that the same gods that they had all worshipped before had answered their prayers.

The money now arriving was the equivalent of over a million pounds a week in today's values. It was impossible for them to buy, ship and organise the distribution of grain so all their only answer was to distribute their relief in money. Unfortunately this did have the outcome of driving the price of grain up but on the other hand it did have the effect of releasing greater stocks of the commodity. In this province Dollars and Dimes were not known; the only two currencies being pieces of silver and copper cash each having a different value by weight. This was further complicated by the fact that a pound was subdivided into ounces – sixteen to the pound in the cities and large towns but twenty in the smaller villages. Even the cash had problems. In one place eighty-two was considered to be a hundred, in another, fifty and another sixteen. There were *cash* shops where you could buy brass coins inscribed with Chinese characters and with a square hole in its centre so that they could be threaded a hundred at a time on a piece of straw twist. These shops were notoriously unreliable as they categorised *cash* into spurious *cash,* small *cash,* wanted *cash* and each string would have to be checked for content when traded with the usual haggling when any alleged small *cash* was found. The blacksmith was kept busy hammering out the silver ingots into one inch squares a quarter of an inch thick to act as coinage. Often when used as currency whoever you might be paying would try to get a better deal by first putting it into the palm of one hand and then transferring it to other before finally declaring that the "touch" was bad and that it was inferior silver. The pace of work gradually sapped Timothy's strength and eventually he contracted dysentery This then meant that he had to leave his work and be carried on a litter back to P'ing-yang and then on to Tai-yuan [the capital and largest city of Shanxi Province]. Before he left he refused all requests to provide him with gifts making sure that all understood that any money should be spent on the poor. It was normal for anyone who had benefited the community to be given a very large red umbrella signed by all those affected. In spite of this the local gentry insisted on erecting a stone tablet with the inscription "What benefice and grace does this display on the part of his August Majesty the Emperor of China, that men should come from the ends of the earth to succour and aid his people". A deputation also insisted on taking a photograph of him and his assistants to hang in their temple. Finally the Governor sent him a very flattering letter of thanks, which Timothy later destroyed in case he was tempted to use it for personal gain. Later in the year he was offered an official rank, something that was unknown for a non-governmental representative. This too he declined in case it set him apart from those he was trying to help.

9 – The Dawn of a new beginning

Having been warmly accepted in Shansi Timothy was now convinced that there was a strong need to establish Christian Missions and to start the ball rolling he wrote to the China Inland Mission [C.I.M.] requesting further help. Three intrepid ladies joined them – the first European ladies to travel so far inland. One Mrs Hudson Taylor immediately set to work helping the orphaned children. Her husband later on was the cause of some friction with Timothy when he started to argue about the way he was running things eventually stating that he did not wish to embark on any further joint ventures. Mrs James arrived with her husband – he was later to be brutally killed in the Boxer uprising in Peking- all of them were to set up and live in Timothy's house whilst he visited the coastal regions.

He had also come to the conclusion that he needed a partner to share some of his responsibilities and had for some time been meeting a Mary Martin who had been sent out from Scotland to help with missionary work in Chefoo. Charming, an intellectual, musical but with a firm practical mind she willingly accepted Timothy's proposal of marriage. After a brief engagement they married in October 1878 and then set out back to Tai-yuan-fu in November. Timothy now felt that he had a home, something he had not felt since he left Wales. He was disappointed to find that the members of the China

Inland Mission were still living in his house as they had not succeeded in obtaining rented accommodation. However it was perhaps to the good, as he soon had to leave their company whilst he went to southern Shansi to finalise the distribution of famine relief.

Having now felt that he had gained the respect of the majority of the population in the area by the distribution of material items his mind turned to what he obviously thought was his main reason in being there – the spread of Christian teachings. He managed to obtain a complete set of Roman Catholic publications that had been translated into Chinese, also from Peking came a set of those of the Greek/Russian Church.

The Jesuit priest Ricci and his colleagues had lived from 1600 as Court Astronomers and had developed close bonds with the Emperor and his officials. Working together they developed the written works of Christianity, which in turn brought many converts from the highest circles into their fold. This in turn brought further followers from the masses that were forever seeking guidance and enlightenments. Ironically it was bitter sectarianism within the church that prevented them from laying the foundation of Christianity in China. Having gained access to these Catholic gems he was not going to make the same mistakes as Protestant literature was still hard to find. The early Christians had frowned upon ancestor worship but as it was a powerful tool in the uniting of families and clans Timothy was not inclined to dismiss it quite so easily as he saw it as the cement that bound Chinese society at the time. He felt that any change should be gradually introduced into his teachings and that they should be for the good and that any attack on ancestor worship would be seen as sacrilege in Chinese eyes. For this reason he had to censor the literature he had by removing those items he thought might offend the local inhabitants. Timothy, fortunately, had learnt a lot about the Chinese culture and the way they thought. He was always reminded of a high-minded missionary who set out to impress him when he had just arrived in China, this man had triumphantly brought in an ancestral family icon of a native Christian family. It was very important to their family, but nevertheless he had persuaded the owner that it should be burnt. Timothy's reply was simple; "I trust that you are going to burn all the photos of your family that you have around you at the same time". The tablet remained intact.

Timothy's willingness to work with and in some cases, adopt other religions' values was one of his great strengths. His wife brought up in a strict religiously dogmatic Scottish family had also over the months become more tolerant and pragmatic in her work. This had not gone down well with her brother, a businessman in Liverpool, who tried to remind her that he too had travelled the world and had come to the conclusion that only Christianity brought joy to the masses.

Timothy felt he had to respond to this and he wrote to his brother –in –law pointing out all the missionaries he knew in all the continents of the world who had made greater progress by adapting to local needs and assimilating with local religions and customs, after all, he pointed out, it was the individual that counted and not their dedication to theories.

He now set upon the task of organising his work in China. He was greatly impressed by the Catholics who allocated a different province to each denomination, operating centrally instead of trying to cover whole areas with several missions. These were experimental days with missions feeling their way forward. It was ironic that Christian charity was moving at a faster rate in China with the different bodies uniting in their efforts yet at home they still went their ever-disparate ways. Timothy Richard was a great believer in breaking down the walls that created the divisions between Presbyterians, Congregationalists, Baptists and Methodists

All too aware of the wasted, duplication of effort created by religious dogma he was determined to start a new form teaching to all men.

Carrying out his relief work in P'ing-yang, he found to his surprise, that Christianity had already been quite well established there over a thousand years before. A general, famous in his time, who had fought the Hun and the Turks was, he found out, a Nestorian [Syrian] Christian and had resided in that city. To the South of the Shansi borders lay Loyang, the ancient capital of China and it was chronicled that in the 7th century that as many as 3,000 foreigners were living there with a significant proportion being Nestorian Christians. They built many churches and spread their religion over large parts of China. Their influence gradually diminished over the centuries primarily due to war, persecution and their ultimate assimilation into Buddhism. At the same time Japan sent a deputation of some of its most learned men where they established an embassy. This resulted in a high degree of cross-fertilisation with the adoption by Japan of Chinese literature, manners, customs and religion particularly Buddhism. They carried back also a form of religion, largely Christian that prevailed under the name of Higher Buddhism [Ta Cheng Kiao].

It was in 1879 that David Hill came to live in Tai-yuan for a short time. The friendship that started there was to last until his death. Hill was a rare missionary – he wrote in Chinese character, an accomplishment very few westerners at that time were capable of. Even Timothy was never able to master Chinese writing, always having to dictate to local scholars but he did persevere to the end on simple tracts.

It was around this time that the Shansi missionaries, under Timothy's instruction started to carry their message to every county of the province, this being done by distributing carefully selected literature. This task covering difficult and hostile terrain was accomplished within twelve months. Within that year the triennial examinations to obtain an M.A. degree were underway and again some of these pamphlets proved useful in providing learning and also as prizes. Sir Robert Hart had provided money to encourage the study of Western civilisation and many of the students wrote essays on the subject. This resulted in an increased interest in the Christian doctrine and a consequential prospering of the church in Tai-yan. Being ever resourceful they brought grapes from the north of the province in order to produce Communion wine, relying heavily on the expertise of the Roman Catholic priests who, being Italian were well versed in the art.

Tension was rising between Russia and China and with the possibility of hostilities breaking out, the Governor Tseng was called to the coastal area to help prepare an army. Most of his conscripts disappeared en route being a very raggle taggle bunch of men. Timothy was convinced that any action by the Chinese, who were inadequately armed with only with bows and arrows and muzzle loading guns, would ultimately end in disaster, decided to go Peking and distribute pamphlets urging peace. This brought about an edict from the authorities stating that anyone advocating peace was a traitor and would be punished. Next month he and Jonathan Lees were summoned to Tientsin to see the Viceroy Li Hung Chang who didn't mince his words when he said that basically their Christian converts were reliant on the wages received by either the missions or from local employment. Withdrawal of these wages would mean that there would no longer be any Christians, especially as there were no Christians amongst the educated classes. This last remark hit home with Timothy who resolved that on his return to Shansi he would target the officials, leaders and scholars by holding a series of lectures and discussions on the different religions.

To strengthen their cause he convinced the English Baptists and American Presbyterians not to form separate churches in Tai-yuan but to have one united church, this he then expanded to the work of the missionaries themselves where, to avoid any friction or overlapping of activities, each would define the boundaries of their influence. This initiative was brought to a halt when Mr. Hudson Taylor, of the Inland Mission, ordered his members to have a separate place of worship, as he did not agree with Timothy's religious teachings. The Inland Mission then set up a separate school; this induced Timothy to go to Chefoo to see Hudson Taylor in person in the hope of settling the matter. Hudson Taylor was immovable and in spite of Timothy having been there longer and having set up the organisation for famine relief he refused to back down. Timothy decided that as a point of principle he was not going dilute his and others resources and said that he would allow the school set up by his wife to merge with the Inland Mission. With much sadness Mrs. Richards handed over some sixty pupils to whom she had become much attached especially as the first ten of them had all converted.

Timothy now had time to develop some ideas. His mind, ever active, turned to the idea of publishing the lives of notable Christians in the west – which his wife with the help of a Chinese writer, a Mr. Kao, actively took up. This influenced Mr. Kao to such a degree that he too became a Christian. Timothy now turned to problems of communication and transport. He drew up plans for establishing railways enquiring if the loose surface that turned roads into muddy morasses could stand the weight of a laden iron railroad. He was fascinated by flight and seeing that the Chinese were well advanced in kite flying and design, offered a prize for the first manned kite flight. This challenge, though talked about at length, did not stimulate the Chinese in any way and was soon forgotten after news of Bleriots flight across the English Channel became known.

Up to 1842 foreigners had not been allowed to reside anywhere in China except on a long narrow mudflat just outside Canton. Following the opium war of that year, an island that the Chinese considered worthless, Hong Kong, was ceded to the British together with the five southern ports of Canton, Amoy, Foochow, Ningpo [see map] and Shanghai, which were opened for trading. Towards the north and the centre all was forbidden territory. It took a further twenty years for the northern ports to open eventually giving way to the establishment of foreign legations and residents in Peking, but still the interior was closed to any form of residency. This slow progress was due to the not unnatural anti-foreign sentiment of the government. Having been allowed during previous dynasties the free movement of Hindus, Jews, Partians, Christians and Mohammedans, it took a combination of the Portuguese and Dutch buccaneers posing as traders, the attacks by Japanese raiders and pirates, the claims made by the Catholic church the trade of British opium coupled with the conquest of India to eventually cause the Manchus and Chinese to close their doors and minds to all that was foreign. This was amplified when they learned that the Pope had assumed that he was the sole ruler of the whole planet and that the East was to be given to Portugal and the Americas were to be given to Spain. The Manchu Governments greatest fear was that with the conquest of India – they were the next in line from the aggressive West. The Manchu's themselves assumed that the Son of Heaven was the sole ruler of the world so, when the East India Company arrived in Canton, edicts were issued to Lord Napier, as if he was Chinese subject, requiring him to obey *in fear trembling*. It was this conflict of two similar assumptions that brought about the first war with China.

After the Tai-ping rebellion the Chinese began to fear other religions and to treat all other teachings as religious propaganda, even though treaties of religious toleration had been signed, such was the mood that the government issued instructions to all of their officials that they were to do their utmost to prevent missionaries settling in the interior. This went as far as passing the death sentence on anyone found with any correspondence indicating that they were thinking of renting property to a foreigner. Invariably the opening of almost every mission station in China was accompanied by an organised riot. Timothy's good work was well known, as was his lack of religious forcefulness and edicts. It was for this reason that he had relatively little difficulty in obtaining entry to Shantung and ultimately into Shansi. He now set upon the task of educating the governing classes on the benefits of results obtained from Western research. His aim was to illustrate how the vast natural resources in China, given to them by God, could be exploited for the benefit of all. Coupled with this he also wanted to show that in modernising an economy changes were required to be carried out, communications especially roads, had to be improved.

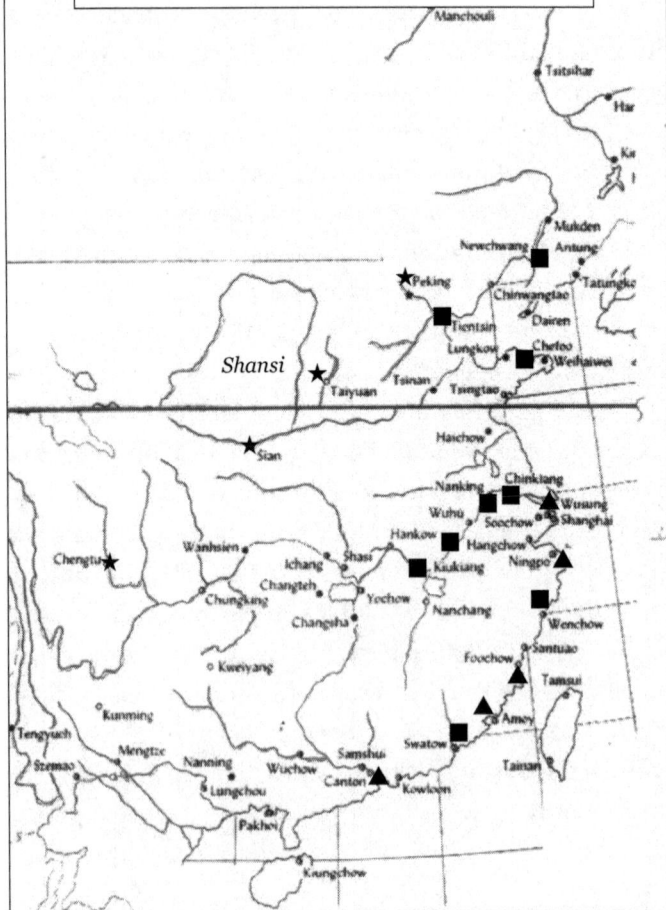

CHINESE TRADING CENTRES
1858 – 1920

★ Important Centres

● Other ports and trading centres 1920

■ Treaty ports open by 1858

▲ Original Treaty Ports 1842 – 1844

Manchouli

Tsitsihar

Har

Ki
I

Mukden
Newchwang Antung
Tatungko

★Peking Chinwangtao
Tientsin Dairen
Lungkow Chefoo
Tsinan Weihaiwei
Shansi ★
Taiyuan Tsingtao

★Sian Haichow

Nanking Chinkiang
Wuhu Wusung
Soochow Shanghai
Hankow Hangchow
Wanhsien Shasi Kiukiang Ningpo
Chengtu★ Ichang
Changteh Yochow
Chungking Nanchang
Changsha Wenchow

Kweiyang Foochow Santuao
Tamsui
Kunming Amoy
Tengyueh Taiman
Ssumao Mengtze Nanning Swatow Taiman
Wuchow Samshui
Lungchou Canton Kowloon
Pakhoi

Kiungchow

Before he could start this mammoth task out he had to devote himself to study and to enable him to purchase the equipment needed to carry out lectures and demonstrations both he and his wife lived solely on rice for some months. He spent the proceeds of a legacy given to him by a relative plus virtually all of the £400 a year income he was receiving on books and instruments. The modern student would not now recognise some of the equipment he bought; it most certainly was unknown to all but a fortunate few in China. Besides books on Buddhism in Chinese he bought several other sacred books of the east plus books on science and medicine and the Encyclopaedia Britannica. Of the equipment with which to carry out demonstrations he bought a telescope, microscope, spectroscope, dynamo, a Wimshurst machine [generator]], induction coil, several galvanic batteries together with a galvanometer, Geissler tubes [The tube was invented by a German physicist and glassblower Heinrich Geissler in 1857. The Geissler tube was a vacuum sealed glass cylinder with an electrode at each end containing one or more of the following thinned gasses, such as neon, argon, or air; mercury or other conductive liquids; or ionisable minerals or metals, such as sodium. When a high voltage was applied to the terminals, an electrical current flowed through the tube which created different lighting effects. The light would be characteristic of the material contained within the tube and would be composed of one or more narrow spectral lines]. He also had a voltmeter, electrometer, pocket sextant and pocket aneroids. He then bought "magic lanterns" [projectors] with the light provided by oxyhydrogen, spirits of wine and acetylene. With these he could show the slides that he had on astronomy, his natural history slides on Australia showing animal life that even the vast majority of the British population had not seen and images of America. On botany he would be able to show slides on tea, coffee, cocoa, rubber trees, sugar cane etc. all with the intention of showing the Chinese how they could grow themselves out of poverty and starvation. He even bought a sewing machine to show them how mechanisation could do the work of many and better than any individual.

With all of this equipment he started to give regular lectures to all officials and scholars that requested his knowledge. He lectured on Haley's comet showing its path in the sky and its lack of evil or bad portents – which many believed it was a precursor to. So popular were his lectures that the Manchus and Chinese quarrelled over whether a new theatre they had built should be handed over to Timothy for his sole use. He declined stating that the time was not yet right for such a move.

His demonstrations or "experiments" in Tai-yan and its neighbourhood brought thousands in from many cities and towns and were seen as being truly remarkable, which in a way they were for even in the West such things were rare since electrical development was still in its infancy. What was important though was the fact that his audiences were made very aware that all of his knowledge he had obtained from books. His aim was to show that God provided the means for man to harness the forces of nature to ease their burden.

Among the many visitors he received was a Mr. Wang from one of the central provinces. He had recently been made Prefect of an area in Shansi and during their discussion Timothy asked him if he had made any reforms since he had assumed his post. Mr. Wang then spoke enthusiastically about the new school he had established in which modern science was being taught but not to such an advanced nature that he had just seen Timothy demonstrate. He also made the comment that he was surprised that as a Buddhist he had learnt that Christians like Timothy also believed in a heaven and hell.

Hanging on the wall of his study was an astronomical map of the solar system. Timothy pointed to the planets and asked Mr. Wang if he knew that their strength of gravitation and the pressure of their atmosphere was dependent on their size and that if we were to travel to them we would either be crushed by the weight of the atmosphere or explode, therefore we had to change or apply something in or around our bodies in order to survive. Mr. Wang nodded in agreement. Timothy then asked if he had ever rewarded the best boys in his school and why. "Yes we do in order to encourage them" came the reply. "So have you also pulled down your jail?" he asked. "No because those contained within if released would only do harm to others" replied Wang. Timothy made the comment that as a mandarin Mr. Wang was well versed in the principles of rewards and punishment and that God himself had to operate with same principles.

This conversation had a great effect on Wang and as he rose he said that if their conversation were printed then no Confucianist would quibble or split hairs at Christianity.

Around 1880 Timothy had an interview with the Viceroy Tso Tsung-t'ang, China's foremost general. He and his army were famous in contemporary Chinese history. Sent to crush the Western Mohammedans and return the great Central Asian state of Ili to the Emperor's control he succeeded by making his men farm during the summer and then sent them plus any extra volunteers to campaign during the autumn and winter. On his way back from one such campaign he sent out an emissary to Timothy to suggest that they met. By chance Timothy had just completed an historical chart of the world for use by ordinary Chinese to get a better grasp of the world's history. He took this as a present to the Viceroy who, after receiving the officials asked for a private audience with Timothy that went on late into the night. During this discussion Tso showed Timothy the variety of woollen products from a mill he had had been built by foreigners in Kansu. After explaining his role in famine relief in the area Tso insisted that there should not be any antagonism between Confucianism and Christianity. Soon after Tso became Viceroy of Nanking and broke down the barriers that had made the building of Christian based schools difficult.

With both Timothy and his wife becoming increasingly drawn into the Chinese society and way of life they both became very interested in Chinese music. To his amazement he discovered that the Chinese already had in place a Tonic Sol-fa system very similar to the European method that had touted as being a breakthrough in the 19th Century. Evidently it was introduced by the Tartars to China around the 10th Century. The only difference being that it did not possess a "key" note as every first note was "Ho".

Such was his knowledge of the music and the instruments used, that when he was invited to attend a rehearsal at a newly constructed temple the sound produced was so bad that the orchestra had to stop. Timothy ventured to suggest that maybe each of the instruments needed to be tuned to which the music master replied that while he agreed but did not know how to carry out such a task. Here Timothy's wife stepped in and managed to bring about a certain amount of musical harmony for which the music master could not thank her enough. It is unlikely that any other foreigner would have been welcomed in a Confucian temple let alone be allowed to tune their instruments.

His influence in Shansi grew by the day such that he was able to ensure better understanding of the safety and welfare of all missionaries and their converts. As officials that he mixed with were promoted to higher posts they were only too pleased to provide him with letters of introduction to smooth the way of missionary work. He now wished to have a better understanding of Buddhism and was allowed to stay a month in one of their chief local temples. Also residing there was an Abbot who had come from one of their main centres to ordain over a hundred priests. He and Timothy always had their meals together. What surprised Timothy was how little training these novices had. It lasted only fifty days, after which they received a diploma stamped by the Abbot. It was clear that an educated monk was a rarity and from his enquiry it appeared that less than one monk in a thousand could even read the diplomas let alone understand what they meant. His next journey took him to one of the most famous Buddhist centres in China – the mountain of Wu T'ai Shan. Within a few days he was at the base of this mountain which rose over 3,600 feet above sea level and on its slopes stood over 150 monasteries [Monks] and lamaseries [Lamas]. Monks of two different Buddhist sects occupied these; one sect from China dressed in grey robes whilst the others, lamas, hailed from Tibet and Mongolia and were dressed in red or were robed in yellow.

Once every year they all came together for a religious gathering, which also incorporated a large horse and mule fair.

On his arrival to witness these proceedings Timothy immediately sent the Abbot his card of introduction and a gift of the map of the world that he had drawn up with all the main countries named in Chinese characters. The two men had a lengthy discussion during which Timothy stated that he had come to study the Buddhist religion and that he would be most grateful if he was allowed to be at worship the following day. The Abbot had no hesitation in granting this request, as he was only too willing to have a westerner expand his understanding of Tibet and Mongolia.

The next day saw Timothy struggling to get through the crowds of Chinese and Mongols as they lined the 108 steps that led to the temple court. Spaced evenly along the steps were servants with whips evidently waiting for him as they cleared a passage through the thronging mob using their whips until his way was clear to enter a large courtyard and then he went through another crowd to a raised platform on which sat a Chinese official and a Mongol official and his wife, all dressed in bright red and yellow robes. With a sweep of the hand the Chinese official invited him to sit next to them in a chair provided.

The worship started with progressively louder beatings of a great drum with musical accompaniment gradually being phased in then prayers followed by a number of priests with deep resonant bass voices – suddenly, unexpectedly, a troop of men emerged wearing masks some modelled on tigers others on bright plumaged birds. It reminded Timothy of similar depictions he had seen in Egyptian mythology. When the dancing was finished he was then ushered into a totally contrasting environment where everything was being carried out with extreme reverence to the background sound of something akin to the Gregorian chants. Two groups each side of an aisle and led by a priest carried out this worship. One group stood with their palms pressed together in front of their face singing in unison a verse of about four lines, whilst the other group prostrated themselves in silence. At a certain point they stood up and the process reversed. Timothy memorised the chant and used the music later in Christian worship.

11 – ONWARDS Towards Peking

In 1882 Chang Chih-tung became Governor of Shansi. He was regarded as one of the great scholars of his time but unfortunately for him he was also in opposition to Prince Kung who was attempting to build stronger ties with foreigners. Chang however, was a patriotic and benevolent man, at one time a millionaire he died penniless having given all his money away for his people's welfare.

Timothy saw little chance of modifying Chang's views on foreigners even if he did allow or tolerate their presence in Shansi. Timothy started to meet him with increasing regularity and offered him various publications. All of this must have had some effect for when the Boxer uprising took place he made sure that as Viceroy of the Yangtse he repeatedly protected the foreigners within his area to the best of his ability, even managing to persuade the "Last Empress" Dowager [Cixi] and her government to moderate her views.

On elevation to Governorship, Chang had brought to him documents discovered in the archives and written by Timothy to the former Governor Tseng suggesting the building of railways to transport the contents from proposed open cast mines to new industrial centres and to set up a college to educate the population on these new techniques and opportunities. This so impressed Chang that he sent a deputation to Timothy to try and persuade him to give up his missionary work and enter the Chinese civil service to carry forward these ideas. Timothy found this a difficult situation and pointed out that he was a visionary and not an expert. He would therefore have to employ foreign experts to carry out this work but in any case his main priority was still to carry out his missionary work. Chang said he fully understood his dilemma but as a favour could he carry out a survey and make some suggestions about the land around Tai-yuan where there were regular floods that affected the livelihood and often took the lives of those housed in the city. This Timothy with, the help of Dr. Schofield, carried out and together with sketch maps and photographs reported back to the Governor together with estimates of the machinery required to carry out the task. Unfortunately, before he could do anything Chang was suddenly made Viceroy of Canton in order to deal with the French who were inflaming border tensions with Annam with the result that it ultimately became a French protectorate.

This work was not wasted for he took the plans with him and when he was made Viceroy of Wuchang he actually built steelworks, railways small industries, set up a modern college and still tried to get Timothy to enter his service, which, again was declined.

Timothy, firmly believing in breaking down the religious barriers between Catholics and Protestants had helped to prevent the Catholic Cathedral in Tai-yuan being pulled down by the locals who were scared that the golden angel on top of the spire was a sign of bad omens since it faced in the direction where the rain clouds always came from and was thus inviting storms to flood the area. The Governor, being inclined to support the locals sent his secretary to Timothy seeking what he thought would be a natural anti-catholic ally, when he got no support and instead returned with a statement that the angel was no more than decoration and not an evil sign he, Timothy, would be very displeased if he did not have the full support of the Governor on the matter and so the cathedral was saved. He also gave sewing machines to the Catholic girl's orphanage when requested to do so and regularly visited their conferences.

In 1882 he was forced to make the journey to Shantung when one of his colleagues had to return to England. The journey was terrible. Travelling in a springless cart for twenty one days the heat was so intense that even his driver declared that it was raining fire. He took with him his Chinese manuscripts with the intention of having them printed when he arrived. No sooner had he handed them over when he became ill with the dreaded dysentery. Daily he became more ill until even he was convinced that he would die. He was so convinced that he sent out messages instructing where to send his body for burial. This alerted Mr. Kitts, the missions' medical expert, who rushed to Timothy covering what would normally have taken three days in half the time only to fall ill to the disease himself when he arrived. Another colleague, Whiteright, arrived as back up but he too became infected. Eventually Mrs. Kitts herself arrived and fortunately, remaining disease free, managed to nurse all three men back to life. The Governor of Shantung, on hearing of the plight of the three, sent an official and his own medical expert with instructions that they were to remain until everyone had recovered. When Timothy called in to thank him he found that he also was to be given an escort for him and his party all the way back to Ch'ing – chou –fu.

He spent that autumn visiting the various churches spread over the counties – churches he had helped set up. In one was a man called K'u who Timothy had only met on three or four occasions but on whom he had made a lasting and deep impression. It emerged as he spoke to the various congregations that K'u had returned from meeting Timothy and started to preach the Christian message in the street. Thinking that he was about to start an uprising everyone rushed home and bolted their doors and windows in case the authorities thought that they were part of it. K'u carried on walking the streets, preaching and since those who hid behind their doors were more or less a captive audience they had no option but to listen to him, gradually they began to take an interest in what he was saying so that ultimately there were five churches built in the area. Whiteright went on to establish a museum which became a popular venue for lectures and teaching symposiums. This was eventually moved to Chi-nan-fu in 1904 where it became even larger with daily lectures and religious addresses being carried out.

Things did not always go smoothly and he was still exposed to officials that were determined to trip him up. He had rented a house in what he considered a good street with absolutely no opposition, when a newly appointed magistrate came to see him. He was told, to his surprise that he must give up his house and seek another as the locals had complained about his presence. Eager to comply Timothy said he would do so but he would appreciate if the magistrate could secure him another place. The magistrate replied that a man as well known as Timothy should have no problem in securing another house and in any case he would give him his full support. Timothy then went back to his own office obtained and then handed over the rental contract. As assumed by the magistrate he immediately found another place and got the two next-door neighbours to sign their agreement on the contract. No sooner had he done this when the same magistrate appeared claiming that the owner, a widow, had not realised what she had done and unless he gave up the contract she would commit suicide. The magistrate also put pressure on Timothy by saying that if the "rabble" got to hear of it they would more than likely set fire to the house. Sussing out that this magistrate was intent on making things as difficult as possible, having first checked that his neighbours did not in fact have a problem, Timothy told him that unless within two days he gave his assent to the transaction, he would put the matter in the hands of his very good friend the consul. When the two days had passed Timothy's cart was ready at the door. As Timothy thought, the magistrate arrived as well but to his surprise did not give in to his wishes. Instead he demanded the return of the contract. Timothy was then forced to travel for eight days to Chefoo where the consul put the case before the Taotai, who ruled about thirty counties, and who promptly issued a proclamation censuring the magistrate.

On his return Chi'ng-chou Timothy was now met, to all intents and purpose, by his new found friend – the magistrate, declaring he would do all he could to make his stay welcome. He asked Timothy if he would show him how his magic lantern worked and within hours of him leaving another deputation of the local gentry appeared requesting that he gave them a lecture involving this magical apparatus each time he held them. His lectures were now virtually a sell out

During the winter months Timothy occupied himself by holding regular Bible Study meetings. As the popularity of these sessions increased he was only too pleased when an old acquaintance offered to help and this gave him a break which enabled him to return to see his wife in Shansi.

Timothy and his Wife Mary

On the journey back some robbers crept in to his room as he slept in an inn, all they found and took was a tin of condensed milk that they evidently mistook for a silver ingot. The good news when he arrived at Tai-yuan was that he was a father of another baby girl, now seven months old, his third daughter.

In that August another good friend, who had helped many times, Dr. Schofield, died from typhus. At the same time the style of governance was changing in the country as the more warlike brother Prince Ch'un succeeded the wise and pragmatic Prince Kung who immediately picked a fight with the French that soon escalated into further anti foreign skirmishes throughout the land.

Having just managed to get over the Taiping anti Christian rebellion and with a Franco-Chinese war now in the ascendance, feelings against foreigners were running rife, especially where it gave free reign to the many who objected to what they saw as alien religions insidiously creeping into their society. This opened the floodgates for those in control who had hidden their true feelings and let rip with a wave of persecutions. This started of with the robbery, imprisonment and abuse of native Christians ultimately spreading to missionaries and their buildings. Only one man stood up and reported to the throne that the troubles were not caused by the foreigners but by the treatment issued by the governing officials and he was Governor of Fukien.

The Baptist Missionary Society belatedly asked Timothy and a recent addition from head office, Huberty James, to become its representatives and to report the state of affairs to the British minister residing in Peking,

Sir Harry Parkes. On arrival they found that the great man had left for Korea in order to ratify a treaty with the Emperor. To make use of their time while they waited for his return, they decided to attempt to form some sort of alliance amongst the missionaries themselves. Eventually they managed to find a form of words – a statement – that all could agree to as a creed to work to. It is interesting to note that the following proclamation had been issued in 1864 by the then Korean Government, which at the time was a part of China. This indicated that they had done some research on the work of Catholic missionaries and it certainly shed some light on how they viewed these people and their teachings.

"1. That God was to be served by virtue and not by begging favours and forgiveness of sins.

2. That God was a Spirit, but Jesus Christ was a man among men.

3. That priests affirm that the soul was more important than the body. As they are the teachers of men's souls they must be obeyed rather than the parents and teachers of men's bodies.

4. That ancestral rites, which existed for the purpose of showing gratitude to ancestors and keeping them in memory, were forbidden by the foreign priests.

5. That the Pope claimed supreme obedience over and above that given to rulers; he was therefore like a robber or rebel disturbing the peace of nations.

6.   That God had created mankind male and female, but the priests exhort celibacy, paid no proper reverence to prince and father, nor due regard to husband and wife.

7.   That the teachings about Holy Virgin, spiritual fathers, baptism, confirmation and salvation were lies to deceive the people.

8.   That since Jesus died miserably, Christians must be drunk or mad to say they fear no death."

Whilst this attitude was prevalent, across the sea a less arrogant society in Japan was forging ahead. Timothy together with Sir Robert Hart desperately tried to convince the Chinese that the only way forward was to grab every able bodied man and set them to task to open mines, improve river navigation, introduce a postal system, establish government controlled banks and to build up a defensive naval organisation. Try as they may they could not convince the powers to be and watched with frustrated dismay as Japan secured more and more power and wealth in the region. The ability to create paid work and the subsequent lessening of the effects of famine gradually slipped out of their grasp.

They gave lectures on the manufacture of cotton goods, the introduction of the Bessemer process to make steel to form rails for the railroads, steel plate to build a navy but all to no avail. Pointing out the success of the Japanese model only brought out a more obstructive attitude from the Chinese.

12 – The first return to Britain

Timothy had now been in China for fifteen years. Most of the time he had spent on his own, pioneering his Christian message to far flung outposts hardly ever visited by Europeans. These last seven years had been easier with his wife giving him support and having a family around him. So in 1884 he found himself with his wife and four daughters on board ship bound for Shanghai.

The city had changed much since he had first landed there in 1869. As his boat passed the Grand Canal entrance at Chingkiang [Zhenjiang] and later its exit further upstream for Tientsin he could view the vast drainage workings on either bank that had been carried out over the centuries and were now being used as commercial waterways. These were linked to another canal that ran for some 140 miles parallel to the Yangtse.

Thousands of boats plied the Lower Yangste ranging from bamboo rafts to junks of every type to sampans, all were part of the distribution network that extended 600 miles inland to the centre of Hangchow – this whole area being labelled the "British Sphere of Influence" – a label that caused some friction and jealousy between Britain's near European neighbours. Obviously the jewel of all this was Shanghai, the so called "Model Settlement of the East". It had grown over a fifty-year period from a modest group of buildings and huts to a massive trading port. Big ships lay at anchor discharging their cargos into smaller lighters and native boats; some would travel further up to Shanghai proper to unload at the wharves. Here there were also moored American three and four masted vessels, also large liners so big that they virtually filled up the dredged channel so that they could only travel in line astern, hence their name. As these massive vessels forced their way against the constant tide of small craft – the air was filled with the sound of sirens and steam whistles.

Passing Soochow [Suzhou] Creek over which a magnificent bridge had been constructed, they came to the British Quarter beyond which again was the French settlement. Going on further were two large permanently moored white hulks that acted as bonded stores for opium, they landed on the British Bund. The Bund was lined with banks, hongs, hotels and large private houses. The most notable buildings were those of the Hong Kong and Shanghai Bank, the P & O offices and the Canadian Pacific Railroad offices but dominant were the offices of the old established firm of Jardine Matheson and Co. All of these surrounded the British Consular buildings and its magnificent garden. Here he met David Jones who had just arrived from England and who was to take over his duties. All was hustle and bustle on the Bund, carriages pulled by one or two horses, open and closed buggies, hundreds of *jinrickshaws,* slowly being referred to as plain rickshaws, wheelbarrows carrying all sorts of cargo – sometimes human, Timothy gave him a quick appraisal of his new surroundings. The "Foreign" area was in stark contrast to the Chinese area, the Chinese certainly appreciated these new developments as they had wide streets, a total absence of rubbish tips and the resultant smells. Consequently there was a demand from the better off Chinese to purchase residences, at a premium, in these quarters He gave Jones a brief lesson on the layout of Shanghai. On the other side of Soochow Creek was Hongkew, the American settlement, very commercial, the French Bund was a continuation of the British Bund – smaller and slightly inferior with less impressive buildings but here laid the very large wharves from which all those steamers that had not chosen the cheaper alternative of discharging further downstream, unloaded their cargoes. The French considered their area more of a colony and not a settlement. This attitude was to be a constant source of friction with the Chinese government. The Franco – Chinese war was starting to escalate, so the timing for Timothy was fortunate but not so for Jones. Onboard he met up with a Buddhist bookseller, Mr. Yang, with whom he started, what was to be a long and fruitful friendship. Yang had been to Europe several times and had met several famous Orientalists, Max Muller from Oxford, Julien of Paris and Bunyo Nanjo a Japanese scholar living in England. This was the ideal springboard for Timothy to resume his study on Buddhism on his return a religion he was beginning to believe that if stripped of its extravagances, it would be the only one likely to rival Christianity in its endeavour to convert the world by peaceful means.

All went smoothly aboard the S.S. Ajax until they entered that well known turbulent Bay of Biscay. With storm force ten and above the captain of the ship had to use his skill trying to keep the vessel afloat – all passengers were confined below decks for three days until a patch of blue sky brought them some welcome relief and then at last, the wonderful sight of the white cliff southern coastline.

Having rested for a few days Timothy was then faced with the task of giving a speech at Exeter Hall. It did not go as well as he had hoped. When he was called it was already late in the afternoon and the vast majority of the audience had melted away to catch their various forms of transport home. Timothy had assumed that it was his speech that was at fault, only to find out later that most of the audience simply had to catch the last train. He was heartened the following week when *The Christian World* ran a leader on his pioneering work in China explaining how he had changed the face of missionary work. Word had also got back that the Baptist Mission was receiving more enquiries and converts than any other Protestant mission.

He was called on again to give his vision on how to spread Christianity in China. Timothy proposed that they concentrate on the educated classes by setting up colleges and then step by step establish higher grade colleges and ultimately a university. His strategy was to begin in the Maritime Provinces where it would be easier to influence the leaders of the Empire to accept Christianity and thereby get them to bring the masses into the fold. His rational was simple, China had a burgeoning population but the mandarins and educated classes only numbered about 100,000, a number that would be manageable and supportable.

The Baptist Society gave this proposal much thought and discussion but came to the conclusion that they simply did not have enough funds to support it. Needless to say Timothy was bitterly disappointed. How do you convince people so far from the reality of what was going on as to what was required?

He resolved to improve his own education so that he could carry out his vision more effectively with minimal interference and financing. He now closeted himself away swatting up on the latest sciences, took a course at South Kensington and sought the help of the Minister of Education. This too backfired. The Minister, an extremely tall man, listened to Timothy's proposals and then suddenly stood up, towering over all in the room, bellowing – "When you have educated these people is it your intention to come back and do the same for ours?" Fortunately, the Vice-President of Education, convinced that Timothy was right, gave him all the information he needed.

It was now time to return to China and leaving their two elder daughters to attend school in Sevenoaks under the careful eye of Mrs. Richard's brother and his wife, who being childless undertook their duties with enthusiasm.

This time they left with their two youngest on the s.s Oxus, a French mail steamer.. He found himself surrounded by Catholics, one young man in particular was very enthusiastic and placed Roman Catholic books on every chair throughout the day. Timothy, sitting and watching this take place over the first few days, eventually called the young man over and said that as Christians they should work together and not try spreading their respective beliefs by propaganda especially when it contained certain elements that were untrue. The young man, visibly shocked at this attack, given in such a kindly tone asked Timothy if he was aware as to whom he was talking to. When he was told that he had no idea whatsoever he stood up and loudly declared in no uncertain tones to Timothy that he was speaking to the President of the Jesuit College in Rue de Bac, Paris and that he certainly was not aware that he was spreading any lies or false statements. Timothy then produced one of the pamphlets that were being circulated – *A short Way with the Protestants*- and told him "I am a Protestant and I can read French and I am telling you that this document contains a number of errors that I am quite willing to sit down with you and discuss."

The young man was adamant that there could not be any errors as he had regularly had discussions every week at his college on Catholicism and Protestantism.

"But did you ever have a Protestant present to state their position?" asked Timothy. The young man, Pere Simon, sheepishly admitted that they had not.

Years later – eleven in fact- Timothy on returning to Shanghai, found a card on his table. Pere Simon was to be consecrated as a Bishop and had invited Timothy to the ceremony. Three months later he died of a heart attack.

Some years later, as part of his belief in cross-denominational activities, he went to see a Jesuit educational institute in Siccawei. The head there, Pere Boucher, whilst taking Timothy and his wife around and showing all that was going on, walked them past a photograph of Bishop Simon. Timothy declared what a good man he had been, "Yes" he replied "He never forgot the talk he had with you on the S.S. Oxus, and ever since then we have kept track of you."

They had not yet reached Shanghai, when Timothy's wife went down with a particularly chronic form of dysentery, at that time considered to be fatal. After receiving a couple of weeks treatment in Shangai, it was considered that she had improved slightly, so they decided to travel to Shansi in the hope that the clearer air there would revive her. As each month passed she became gradually weaker. No medicines seem to have any effect. Just by chance a Dr Edwards arrived and lent Timothy a new book on the subject of dysentery and one of the treatments specified was to stop all food other than milk and to administer it at the rate of one wineglass every hour. To everyone's amazement within the month she had completely recovered.

He now had another problem to overcome. During his absence in England and while he was preoccupied with the welfare of his wife, new inexperienced colleagues had arrived and they had given in to the old jealousies of the other Missions who had totally disagreed with Timothy's methods of working. He was now faced with a revolt within his own ranks – they had been made to agree that the adoption of science was heathen and that any fraternisation with the Catholics was not even to be considered. His main critics refused to come to see him and in the end, with a heavy heart, he was forced to leave Shansi. He packed up all of his belongings with the exception of his scientific apparatus. These items he sold at a great loss to those educated Chinese that he had managed to teach to use them. To his critical colleagues he gave them his magic lantern and slides in the hope that they would make some use of them. He did not even have time to see the Roman Catholic Bishop who lived about three miles away, instead he sent him a farewell note. Within hours the Bishop was round to see him just as he was packing up his books, which were all, scattered around the room. Timothy asked him to look at them and choose one as a memento of their ability to work together. He wrote his name in the book " *Those Holy Fields*" shook hands and parted. The next time Timothy was to hear of him was during the Boxer revolution when the Governor Yu Hsien oversaw the massacre of all missionaries, Catholic and Protestant together with their family's men, women and children in the city, amongst them was the Bishop.

In the October Timothy and his family moved to Tientsin where he was offered a post with the Government as a translator at the very good salary of £600 per annum. Deciding that he could not give up his missionary work he decided that they should move again to Peking where he set up residence in the house vacated by an American Bishop. Here he started his teaching again only to receive from London a communiqué suggesting that he return to Shantung. This he agreed he would do if they would allow him to establish a Christian college at Chi-nan-fu, the capital. Whilst waiting for a reply, he carried on discussions with the leading statesmen in Peking and wrote a pamphlet for distribution comparing the progress of different nation states. In this pamphlet Timothy suggested that the Chinese Government should start a programme of educational reform and should with immediate effect and, to show their commitment, set aside a budget of a million taels annually to fund it.

The local governor replied to Timothy that this amount could not be afforded and when Timothy told him that this was the seed corn from which a rich and prosperous crop would grow and return the investment a hundredfold, he asked over what period of time would they start to see the benefits.

When told it could take up to twenty years to change the current system by training new tutors with new ideas and watching the new students flourish with their new global knowledge, he was told that this was too long, nevertheless many years later he met a Hanlin in charge of a provincial college who had received a copy of his pamphlet and who told him that many progressive administrators such as he had in fact tried to introduce Timothy's ideas as suggested.

This period was a very dark one for Timothy and his wife. Having to move from Shansi, misunderstood, misrepresented and mistrusted by the majority of their colleagues, their only support was actually coming from the Chinese converts who basically loved them for all the good the couple had done over the nine years that they had been married. They spent their anniversary shivering and damp in a run down wayside inn. Eventually they arrived in Peking, where his wife set up a school teaching English to Japanese students. One of these was the son of a Japanese minister who asked Timothy if he would see his father as he wished to become a Christian and needed his permission. This was fortuitous as the Japanese minister in turn introduced Timothy to Marquis Tseng, the first Chinese minister in London who after eight years abroad begged Timothy to let Mrs Richard to teach his son. This grew into a deep friendship during 1888 where Timothy could supply him with information that he could not get from official sources. He too was also an advocate of railway construction and lobbied hard for a line to be built between Peking and Tientsin. Prince Ch'un asked the Marquis what effect the introduction of the railways had on coachmen and cabmen in and around London. Timothy being the only one able supply this information gave detailed figures and dates. As fate would have it the Marquis died in 1890, again the path of modernisation within China fell from the grasp of those who wanted to move forward.

Timothy now decided to visit the chief lama of Tibetan Buddhism in Peking, this being the prevalent form of Buddhism at that time had spread with the nomadic tribes from Tibet to the Pacific seaboard. Having had experience of the savagery of the Mongol Lamas before, Timothy sent his card together with a gift of an electric bell to the chief lama. Maybe the fact that they did not know how to operate this piece of mechanism was one of the reasons why he was quickly invited to meet him and with the newly arrived John Shorrock they were warmly received and they both soon managed to connected a battery and lay a length of wire from the bell, now positioned in the lama's servants room to the button placed on the arm of the Lama's seat. On pressing the button the servant ran in shouting he could hear it. This amusing session was repeated several times with the lama expressing his delight at such a convenient method of summoning his servant. Following their meal together Timothy found that Lamaism was on the wane in and around Peking and that his time was mainly used now to conduct political rather than religious dialogue.

Come spring he decided to visit Japan to see how the educational proposals he had made that had to date had been shunned by the Chinese and his own Baptist Missionary Society, had progressed and what had happened where they had been taken up by his more enlightened colleagues. Again, on his return, he attempted to have his policies adopted in China; again they were refused as being "too radical". He now considered severing his ties with the Baptist Society, David Jones on hearing this wired him from Ch'ing-chou begging him not to carry out this threat and in fact came to see him to ask him to re-join the Shantung Mission. In that September Timothy arrived there and laid down his terms These amounted to a demand that he would be allowed to establish a Christian college at Chi-nan-fu, aided by at least ten evangelist assistants.

It was now May 1889 and another famine was affecting Shantung. Timothy, at the behest of his colleagues moved out of Peking to Tientsin and then set out on his own for Shantung. Working with his promised assistants he started the famine relief projects again around the capital Chi-nan-fu. Famine fever was now rife and he too became a victim. His recovery was slow with his right arm becoming paralysed and very painful. His wife, still weak from her illness, was instructed on medical orders to rest at the seaside resort of Chefoo – Timothy was also instructed to join her.

Here he wrote a letter to his daughters at home which encapsulated the problems that faced the poor people in the area.

June 14, 1889

"It is now two months and a half since I left Tientsin, where your mother and Florrie and Maggie are, and I have been all this time in the Famine District. That part of it where I have been giving relief to the poor sufferers is about 300 miles from the sea-coast. I propose to give you some account of it in this letter. Some eight years ago the Yellow River, one of the greatest rivers in the world, broke its banks and flooded no less than seven counties in this region. The water was like the sea breaking in, all over the country, sweeping away men, women, children, horses, cows, trees, mules houses and even villages by the rushing flood, carrying everything with it towards the sea. After a time the flood subsided, and where there was once a rich country full of waving corn and splendid orchards and happy homes and villages, now there remained but ruined houses; the whole country was covered as far as the eye could see with nothing but sand left by the floods, and the temples which once stood on high ground in villages and towns were about the only buildings that had not fallen before the flood. The temples are also as a rule better built with brick and mortar, and therefore could withstand the force of the water better than most houses. But the strange thing about these temples now is that they are all buried in sand, some halfway up the doors, some as deep as the tops of the windows, and some even beyond the eaves of the roofs. So temples and God are buried together!

But there were a few patches where the people could cultivate a little land mixed with much sand. So the people that were rich and had the most land were now among the poorest in the land. The people were loath to leave their old land although it was almost useless and in many cases utterly so. Where could they go? China is so full of people everywhere that the poor people did not know what to do. Many tried to get work in the surrounding towns and villages where the floods had not reached, and thus lived from day to day on the earnings of the day. Further on the sand is very fine, and when the wind blows it drifts like snow before the wind. Sometimes it is carried high into the sky in thick dust-clouds, and sometimes-carried away ten, twenty or even a hundred miles off! So the people live in hope that in about eight years, if there is no more flooding of the Yellow River, then much of the sand will be blown away and they could recover their land again! That is why they cling to their old buried villages and towns. But they have been repeatedly disappointed. The Yellow River has broken its banks many times since the first flood. Last year there was an unusual fall of rain all over a very large part of the province, say about thirty counties. The crops rotted in the water. When in addition to the seven counties formerly flooded by the Yellow River, the surrounding twenty odd counties were suddenly deprived of their harvest, this made a great famine all over this part of China.

The English missionaries sent letters to England. American missionaries wrote to the United States to ask for money to save these people from starvation. Benevolent people in England and America subscribed large sums of money. Over twenty missionaries, men and women, were engaged in enrolling the names of the poorest in the towns and villages for regular relief which was given to them once a week, and about 300,000, nearly a third of a million, people were thus receiving regular relief for some time.

You learn from your teachers that wherever there is a famine it is always followed by what is called Famine Fever. It is also called Typhus Fever, and there are various varieties. But usually rich and poor are equally liable to get it. An attack lasts for about three weeks. About a third of those who get it die of it. The rest after about three weeks recover. Your dear mother had this Famine Fever about twelve years ago after the Great Famine which we had then. You will be sorry to hear that though I escaped the Fever that time I did not escape it this time. For some days the temperature of my body ranged between 104 and 105, which is considered very dangerous if it lasts long – few are able to recover from it. But I am thankful to say all the fever has left me now and I am gaining strength rapidly. In about a week I hope to be strong enough to travel to the coast to your mother. She has not known of my illness. I am writing to her today. If she had known, the weather was too hot, the distance too great, and travelling in mule-carts would only endanger her life. Now, however, all is well again. Let God be thanked for His mercy. Be thankful that you live in a land of so many privileges."

This letter encapsulates all the privations that the population and the attendant missionaries had to endure.

Whilst he was recuperating Timothy had a slight change of fortune. All the members of the Ch'ing-chou-fu had made representations to the Baptist Missionary

Committee supporting him in his quest to set up a college in the provincial capital of Chi-nan –fu.

The time and the man were ready for such a move. Timothy was well known; he had access to high office and also had the confidence of ministers and the populace alike. He had just received accolades for his work on Famine Relief. However, his wish to remain a Baptist missionary and to carry out his educational plan was dealt a crushing blow when, having packed all of the family belongings for the journey to Shantung, his medical adviser intervened and insisted that he delayed carrying out any form of exertion. His poor physical condition meant that any long stressful journey would mean a total relapse. He still had trouble moving his arm which made him incapable of writing. He bowed to the advice of his doctor and delayed his departure date.

In the October of 1889 the decision of the committee arrived – this was another body blow – they had not given consent to found a Christian college. He was advised to return to Shantung and realign himself with his fellow brethren there. In order to make a decision that would not upset his peers in case they had the impression that he considered himself in the slightest way superior, he consulted with his friends in Peking and Tientsin and the advice that they gave was to hold out and not accept the proposal offered.

This meant that he had now cut himself off from any form salary from the Baptist mission. Not wishing to give up his work as a Christian missionary he still refused the many offers he received to use his services for networking and translating and utilising his command of the language and customs.

Whilst all this was going on a second General Missionary Conference was being held in Shanghai. These involved delegates from all corners of the British Empire numbering over 400 in addition to those that came from all the Chinese provinces, plus Japan, Korea, Singapore, Burma and Tibet. His work on Famine Relief had prevented him from attending the first conference but this time he was determined to attend. On arrival he was invited to read a paper on "The Relation of Christian Missions to the Chinese Government". He used this to try to prevent the publication by the Chinese of what were known as the Blue Books of China – a part of which contained a chronicle of all the accusations made against the Christian church – mostly false. Timothy was worried that if a cheaper version were to be published it would raise anti-Christian feelings, a concern which unfortunately would later be proven to be correct. After the conference he went to Nanking and then to Tientsin desperately pleading with the Viceroys to suppress these publications. All of his representations were ignored probably because both Viceroys were politically aware that any action taken on this matter would not be well received in Peking. As a way of mitigating these decisions the Viceroy of Tientsin invited Timothy to become editor of a local Chinese daily, the *Shi Pao* or "Times". This was providential as it allowed Timothy a mouthpiece to speak to many thousands of ordinary people. Through this medium he also published a weekly version with articles and coloured maps of the world showing population densities, railways, telegraph stations and the routes taken for the movement of different goods. These articles made some of the Chinese intellectuals realise just how backward China was as a nation. His illustrations created much interest in many parts of the country with copies being ordered by high officials which ultimately found their way into the Royal Palace in Peking.

During 1890 the Russian Tsarevitch [the heir apparent] had travelled to the Far East in order to turn the first sod of earth to signify the start of construction of the Trans-Siberian Railway. He had requested that whilst he was this Far East that he would like to visit Peking, a request that perturbed the Chinese Government. By chance Timothy's latest publication had advocated the visits of high officials to Europe, as those officials in Europe were visiting each other all the time and also journeying to other continents – China was increasingly isolating itself both politically and culturally. His articles certainly helped oil the wheels in the decision making process to receive the Tsarevitch at a state function. In 1890 the Baptist Missionary Society sent out a two-man deputation Dr. Richard Glover and the Rev. William Morris. Warmly received by Timothy these men were to have a major impact on Timothy's future for in 1891 Dr Alexander Williamson – the founder of the Society for the Diffusion of Christian and General Knowledge among the Chinese – died. The Societies' committee met and having seen in Timothy a man with the ideal presence and vision they immediately contacted him and invited him to succeed Dr. Williamson. The downside of the offer was that the Society had little cash and could not offer him a salary since most of their income went on publications. By chance a deputation from the Baptist Missionary Society was visiting China at the same time and, on hearing of their plight offered to support Timothy for three years. In the October of that year Timothy and his wife again moved to Shanghai.

Travelling downstream on the Yangtse meant that they had to hire a boat, this in turn was attached to a long chain of other boats with the largest at the front and they, in their small craft near the rear, all being pulled along by a tow-boat belching black smoke and depositing large sooty smuts on all those behind. As they set off there was a cacophony of gongs being crashed, a sea of flags being waved and the usual crackers exploding. After silence had descended long poles would emerge from the boats with clothes attached to dry in the wind. The sweet smell of incense was all pervading as fires were lit ready to provide night time warmth in readiness for cooking. Each boat appeared to contain a whole family from grandparents down.

On arrival at Shanghai Timothy took up the position of secretary and his first act was to reduce the long and tortuous title of the Society to "The Christian Literature Society of China" and still briefer the C.L.S. He assembled an influential group of men – John Macgregor of Jardine, Matheson & Co. Sir Robert Hart, Sir Charles Addis – soon to become a Governor of the Bank of England – as Trustees, but he was still the only full time member and its only Director.

Little did he know that he was now at the halfway stage of his life in China. During this time he had witnessed great disasters, founded famine relief, embarked on great adventures to regions totally alien to westerners and had founded the Baptist Missions in Shantung and Shansi, he had also unknowingly, come to the attention of the Royal Household who were watching his every move with increased interest.

He gradually secured part time help from such people as Dr. Otto Faber, who possessed that rare combination of being a German with a dry sense of humour. Once when asked where was his thesis on the Christian attitude on Chinese Classics that he had spoken about writing for so long, he replied "It is in the ink bottle". Nevertheless he managed to get it published shortly before he died of dysentery in 1899.

Timothy now sat down to establish his plan. He reiterated his beliefs thus:-

"The generosity of the foreign communities in China and at home has repeatedly been shown in response to appeals for famine relief; but when through ignorance many of the preventable causes of these famines are not removed, there is a growing feeling that the best way to help China is to give such kind of enlightenment as this Society attempts to give. We cannot even *dream* of establishing modern schools throughout the Empire; this will be the province of the Chinese Government after it somewhat understands its own needs and how to meet them. Nor do we intend to reach all the Mandarins in the Empire. Much less can we reach every one of the *literati*, who play such an important part in the government of China. Still, the chief mandarins, together with the High Examiners, Educational Inspectors of counties, Professors of colleges, and a small percentage of the *literati,* with some of the ladies and children of their families, might be reached." At the time this was estimated to be about 44,036!

He now set down to ask other leading missionaries what subject matter they should concentrate on. As a result of this dialogue he secured a list of subjects and, more importantly, the offer of assistance to help in translating the subject matter. The next problem was the cost of printing and distribution. In the past such publications had been distributed by missionaries – Chinese bookshops would not touch them as the Chinese themselves were averse to buying foreign publications which, to them, upset so many of their own long held beliefs and doctrines. He managed to scrape together sufficient funds to enable free distribution of his works at the 1892 Peking Triennial Examinations. He also started to translate a book that was perhaps, the most influential publication at that time but little known now- Mackenzie's *History of the Nineteenth Century*. This became widely read and was to influence the minds of many Chinese academics in favour of reform for when published it was a comprehensive and informative look at the history of the Nineteenth Century and appealed to all historians. It detailed all aspects of the change in the governance and development of Europe from the downfall of the monarchy in France to the rise of Napoléon and the birth of the first republic. It chronicled all the major wars and their effect on history. It then delved into the detail of social reforms in Britain, the growth of industry, the exploitation of child labour and the political reform bills that were passed by parliament. It also did a potted analysis of the history of each country. It was invaluable to scholars but also considered as potentially explosive by the ruling classes, if read by too many people. China at this time was still a slumbering giant. It would not receive its wake up call until a modernised Japan invaded and declared war in 1894.

In 1893 the country was organising itself to celebrate the sixtieth birthday [sixty years in the Chinese cycle] of the Empress Dowager [Cixi]. This was an opportunity that Timothy grasped with both hands. An appeal was launched for all the Christian women in China to donate a sum of money or gifts to enable the presentation of a special copy of the New Testament to be made to her Majesty.

With 1200 dollars at their disposal they printed a most magnificent copy in large type on the best quality foreign paper with an explanatory introduction prepared by Dr. William Muirhead of the London Missionary Society. The whole book was bound in silver coins and made in Canton. The address, prepared by Timothy's wife went as follows :-

Madam, – Your Imperial Majesty having, by Divine appointment, undertaken the government of China in times of unparalleled internal and external trouble, and having by your great energy and wisdom restored profound peace throughout the whole Empire and established friendly relation with all nations, has called forth for the admiration, not only of your subjects, but of those of other nations far and wide.

Among the many just laws which your Majesty has established, not the least is that which commands the same protection to your Christian subjects as to those of all other religions: Therefore we, a few thousand Protestant Christian women throughout the various provinces of your Empire, though mostly poor, cannot let the auspicious occasion of your Imperial Majesty's sixtieth birthday pass without testifying our loyalty and admiration. We do so by presenting your Majesty with the New Testament, which is the principal classic of our holy religion – namely, the religion of Jesus Christ, which is the only religion which practically aims at the salvation of the whole world from sin and suffering. The truths in this volume have brought peace of heart and purity of life, with hope of everlasting happiness, to countless millions. It has also given to Christian nations the just laws and stable government which are at the root of their temporal prosperity and power. On this account we hear it is a custom in the West to present Empresses, Queens and Princesses with a copy of this book on happy occasions in their lives. We Christians in your Empire constantly and fervently pray that your Majesty and all the members of the Imperial Household may also get possession of this secret of true happiness to the individual and prosperity to the nation so that China may not be behind any nation on earth. We also pray that your Imperial Majesty may long be spared to help your wise counsel in the government of China, and that when your work on this earth is finished you may have a happy entrance into the glorious land prepared for all those who carry out the beneficent will of Heaven. We remain, with the profoundest veneration, Madam, your Majesty's most grateful subjects,

The Women of the Protestant
Christian Church in China.

The casket was presented on 11th November 1894 by both the British and American ambassadors via the Foreign Office [Tsungli Yamen]. By a stroke of luck the office delayed passing it on which meant that it was presented to the Dowager Duchess at the same time as a gift arrived from Queen Victoria.

This address with its required obsequiousness was certainly a politically motivated action to open doors and created some format for subsequent dialogue. It was well known that the Empress had risen from humble beginnings to become the Emperor's favourite concubine, fortunately giving him his only son and heir. She was also a formidable woman and had frequent power battles with her husband and on his death had amassed sufficient allies to ensure that of all the other seven regents named by the Emperor she was the one that could seize power.

As she could not openly rule the nation, she had to do it ostensibly through her son from the age of five. This she did right up to the time he reached seventeen when he took over the throne only to die of venereal disease shortly afterwards. Some thought that she ensured his infection by selecting his concubines. There was one more hurdle to jump, her son's favourite concubine was pregnant and if she gave birth to a boy then there would be a different Dowager Empress. Mysteriously this concubine died before giving birth, some again thought on the instruction of Cixi, others thought that she took her own life as she had a history of mental instability.

In due course the Empress Dowager acknowledged the gift by sending rolls of silk to all those ladies involved and also sent a eunuch to Peking to procure a copy of the whole Bible.

In 1893 the government had allowed depots to be established for the sale of literature, this allowed the circulation of Timothy's papers to greatly expand, especially the *International Review* and his *Nineteenth Century*. The following year was one of continuous expansion, many high Chinese officials were now supporting the Society with substantial donations and at the same time Chinese directors of companies were buying the *Nineteenth Century* in their hundreds and then distributing them to leading officials and employees. That same year Sir Thomas Hanbury became the principal benefactor of the Society and provided cash prizes for the best essays on how to improve the infrastructure of the country. He later showed his commitment by leaving a large bequest in his will – sufficient enough to buy land and commence building some imposing offices for the Society. Mr. And Mrs. Archibald Little then approached Timothy and his wife with the idea of founding an Anti Footbinding Society. This practice was widespread in China, although Marco Polo never once mentioned it in his diaries. Timothy immediately allowed the Littles to use his magazines to support their cause, and although there was a Natural Foot Society already in existence, the campaign really took off releasing a pent up wave of public opinion against the painful and often crippling practice, the Manchus funnily enough never bound their feet. Chinese woman used this as a way of liberating themselves and with Empress Dowager on their side; she was a Manchu, issuing an edict exhorting her subjects to abandon the custom Timothy found himself once again being lionised by another part of Chinese Society.

Timothy now recruited a young man J. Lambert Rees into the Society. He was of outstanding ability and Timothy gave him the job of translating an important book published at that time – Lessing's *Education of the Human Race*. This in itself was a massive piece of work and when Timothy returned from one of his travels a few months later he found the work complete and had it printed. Forwarding the first copy to Viceroy Chang Chih-tung he was surprised to receive a request for more copies plus a generous donation that more than covered the printing costs. With the donation was also a request that a history of the world should be brought out. Mr. Rees had by this time returned to the American Episcopal Church but his Archbishop, Graves, allowed him to spend a portion of his time over the following years to carry out this task – the book being published by the Society in 1900 comprising three volumes and similar in size to the Encyclopaedia Britannica of that time. The Viceroy again thrilled at the publication and gave another generous donation plus an order for several copies. This was the most complete universal history that the Chinese had seen to date and was to have further groundbreaking effects on the Chinese education system some ten years later. Now Timothy was in charge of an organisation that was and could be powerful and influential in developing and moulding Chinese society into the modern world.

13 – The Sino –Japanese War

1894 was the second great awakening for China. Its insular policies had gradually been eroded by the western countries breaking down the Chinese' sense of superiority in art, culture and refinement, but now it faced an emerging eastern power – Japan. Having kept the western "barbarian" confined mainly to the coastal areas it was a shock when their despised "dwarf" neighbours started to cast off their traditional clothes and gradually adopt western style dress. It was even a greater shock when they found that Japan had discovered that gunpowder and steel armaments were a far more potent and efficient means of promoting and imposing "civilisation" than the theatre, art and dance.

They had built up a fleet of warships ordered from John Brown Armstrongs in the UK, and with British help raced on to develop and build more Dreadnoughts, [the largest capital ships of the time] cruisers and light cruisers under British supervision. They very quickly made sure that all their ships were powered by turbines and were state of the art. By contrast the Chinese ships were outdated, slow, under armed and rarely left their berths mainly because they had hardly any maintenance carried out and in consequence were totally unreliable.

Japan had always cast its eye over Korea and was fearful that it may come under the control of Russia or one of the western powers thus leaving it very exposed to any aggression from the north. After many skirmishes it had signed a treaty with Japan enabling the opening of some of the ports to trade. This caused concern in China who viewed the country as a tributary state under the influence of the Qing dynasty.

Word now reached them that a British merchant vessel, the *Kow-shing* had been sunk by Japanese naval forces off the coast of Assan. A Chinese cruiser and two gunboats, which had been chartered by the Chinese government to ferry troops and ammunition to Korea, were escorting this ship. It had been intercepted by the Japanese cruiser *Naniwa* and ordered to transfer the European crew members to the *Naniwa*. However, with 1200 Chinese on board threatening to kill the captain if he did so he had no choice but to refuse. The Japanese in turn fired over the vessel allowing most of the Europeans to jump overboard who were then fired on by the Chinese. This act, although not illegal, as it was ostensibly done to quell a mutiny, allowed Japan to declare war on China.

The Japanese now marched on to Seoul, the capital, where they murdered the Queen and then seized control of the country. Now they moved on to Manchuria, heading for Peking. The Empress Dowager sensed that she was now in great danger and had no alternative but to seek foreign assistance. This was readily supplied by Russia who extracted sufficient concessions to lay the foundations for the later Russo- Japanese war.

Timothy at once could see that China, whilst possibly being able to accept the humiliation of being beaten by any western power, simply would not have been able to accept being beaten by a country that was a tenth of her size and up till then she had always patronised.

This is where the S.D.K. made its presence felt. Nearly every month Dr. J. Allen had been writing articles on China's inherent weakness in not building a modern navy. Corrupt officials soon frittered away the money that had been set aside for such projects. The same applied to the building of railways, steamers and telegraph systems, which were essential for a quick reaction to any form of aggression. China had no means of transporting goods or munitions to fend off attacks efficiently neither did it have the means to move food and clothing to needy areas. In short, the Manchus were a pretty useless group of leaders, refusing to recognise their weaknesses and incapable of unlocking the potential that lay in their power for China to become one of the great nations on earth.

Allen wrote that China had been humiliated over the past sixty years simply because the Manchus had obstructed at every level those elements that broke down the barriers between nations, he repeated his mantra – railways, steamers and telegraphs would help promote the integration of nations as it had done in India. Timothy himself was convinced that if China could get its act together it could still become one of the greatest nations on earth.

Booksellers up to this time, had refused to handle Christian literature, but as result of Timothy's widespread issuing and the subsequent reading of the S.D.K. issues by all the educated strata of Chinese society, attitudes had started to change. Indeed, pirated copies of Richard's

Mackensie's History were now on sale with an estimated million copies in circulation. These were fetching three times the amount of the official publications and so the opportunity was taken to increase the prices thus raising the revenue into the S.D.K. which in turn enabled further distribution of free literature to take place. All of this helped start the breakdown of the barriers between western writers and Chinese booksellers.

Timothy now received an invitation to visit the Viceroy in Nanking. Being February – the coldest month on the Yangste – he had a rather difficult journey. He wrote in his diary about the conditions he found in the city and the inn where he spent his first night;

"The day was wet, rain and snow in turns with strong winds. The roads were covered with deep slush, which splashed about with each step; every traveller was doubled up with the cold as if with colic. There was no wheeled conveyance of any kind, but a chair had to be fetched from Hsia Kwah on the other side of the river, for one was not sent to the landing stage where it was wanted. It would have been too much of a shock to conservatism to have it ready on the spot; it must be left where the ancestors kept it, and the chair must the very one used by the ancestors, even to the split boards and ragged calico; and the wind must blow through the very crack which vexed the ancestors. After some half-hour's delay in hunting for the chair-bearers, who are in demand by any steamer that comes, we started.

There are many tumble-down houses on both sides of the streets through which we passed, but what is the most striking to the stranger is the mat sheds on each side. They are about four feet high, seven feet long, and four feet wide. They contain neither table, chair nor bed; the cold ground, covered with a little straw, and a mat, serves for a bed; the only furniture is the cooking pot with a fire under it, and some ragged covering which was once a quilt. The old men and women there cannot resist the cold long, and the scanty food of the young lads brings on disease in their starved frames. Many try to eke out their living by gambling, as they have nothing else to do. Their skins are blue with cold, and broken up with white scales. Their sisters are more fortunate, for they were sold off long ago to a life of comparative luxury – shame some will call it – in order to ward off the day of starvation for their families a few months longer. Terrible as the poverty is, yet Nature asserts herself among those who can no more dream of having a wife than of flying. They occasionally divide their meal with a poor starving widow who is due to have a baby in an adjoining shed, and who for it shares a night's hospitality until the babe comes. But it cannot be reared; it is cast in the night into the cold not fifty yards away, and by the morning the hungry dogs do not even leave the bones behind, only a blood stained rag.

Look at the chair bearers; they are better off, but they have no shoes or stockings; their legs are bare to the knees. They tie on some straw sandals with straw strings and trudge along most happily, ankle-deep in the freezing slush, because they have something to do. They can earn by the slow process of gradual freezing and grafting disease into their system.

We arrive at one of the vice regal inns where high mandarins stay. Instead of having a house of three stories one above the other, these have their space of ground walled round; fronting the street is a house with a front and back door, each about eight feet wide; the front door is only closed at night, the back door is open night and day. Behind this there are two houses like it, each separated by an open court of twenty feet. The entrance to the three is through the one front door. The central part of the hotel has its front and back doors open day and night, the back row alone has only one door open; the back door is walled up, as there are no houses behind. Through these doors the cold wind blows night and day. Then, again, the whole of the front of each row is made up of paper window frames with wide slits between each frame; and the rooms are partitioned off with boards, also with wide fissures between each. As the wind is high it goes through our bedroom like water through a sieve. There is no ceiling, and the partition a little way above one's head connects with a wide passage outside; thus the first-class bedroom is only a roof to prevent the rain and snow falling on one; the winter midnight air has full and free access. This is our first class hotel.

In the bedrooms are two wooden frames which they call beds; they are only bare boards without a thread of bedding. There are also two chairs – only one is usable – a table, and a narrow bench about four inches wide to sit on. On the table is a primitive lamp, probably invented about the time of Abraham. You ask for bedding; they bring a reed mattress and a quilt, damp and greasy, having been used a year without washing. To crown matters, the landlady, with a little girl of six years of age in her arms, comes to the door to give instructions to her husband about the bedding, and the child has measles. They do not see any impropriety in bringing bedding from a house where there is measles. So there is neither warmth nor health nor sleep for one, while he keeps watch on the narrow on his narrow bed and sees his breath rise above him like smoke, because the temperature is far below freezing point.

And this is the condition of society under one of the greatest Viceroys in the Empire. Who will call a Government, which will tolerate such poverty and wretchedness at its very doors, civilized and fit to be put on a par with Christian nations? Such misery of tens of thousands in these mat sheds should melt the hearts of stone to do something to save them."

After this Timothy had two more interviews with the Viceroy. He found that the he had surrounded himself with Chinese who had been trained abroad, but who had gone out with the pre-conceived idea that they were to find out the failings of Western civilization. In this Timothy found a complete lack of statesmanship – an impossibility to see the holistic view that is required in international affairs. It was not surprising then that his view and proposals were not easily accepted. Had they been accepted, then the history of China could have turned out entirely different. He proposed that as China had so much catching up to do, the only fast track route was for a foreign Power to be invited to serve a fixed number of years to look after all of China's foreign affairs, introduce reforms into the country, develop its resources and then hand back a modernised country and society. Timothy recognised that there were two stumbling blocks to this proposal, where would they find this "honest broker" and how would they navigate around the Manchu sovereignty? He also recognised that he was not dealing with the right people. Viceroy Chang's scheme was to send the young princes abroad for education, but as Timothy pointed out by the time they had received it and become worldly wise events could well have overtaken China, his proposal was to send more mature members of the Royal family for a crammed education and have a treaty for foreign alliances to last no more than ten years. But as with all things this was considered too dangerous to present to the Throne.

Timothy did make moves to assist in the start of normalising relations with Japan. The first peace envoy was Chang Yin-hwan, formerly a minister to the United States. He sat down with Timothy in Shanghai to discuss the best of approach. He pointed out the dangers that threatened China through ignorance, and corruption in official circles, and from the threat of revolution fermented by the poverty of the people whilst all the while potentially aggressive foreign countries were keeping a watching brief. This was strong stuff indeed and Timothy suggested that two princes should be sent as Peace Plenipotentiaries to settle the peace terms on a financial basis; that an alliance such as he had suggested to Viceroy Chang be sought; that in the meantime Sir Robert Hart should take up the post of adviser with direct access to the Throne; and that China should seek the support of a Court of International Arbitration.

The Envoy thought long and hard about this and said that he could see that Russia was the power that all others feared, but England was the most reliable and trusted. Timothy pointed out that any joint alliance would bring defeat, but that the alliance should be with one country only. The Envoy again mulled over the proposal and then confided in Timothy that official corruption was on such a grand scale that it was almost impossible to eradicate it and any reform plans put before the government would almost certainly be turned down – even if they could find someone brave enough to present them. He also said that he himself had suggested that members of the Imperial family should be sent abroad but was met with a dull response. He said that China had now succeeded in alienating the few friends that she had and had treated foreign ministers in a most off-hand way and of this he was most ashamed. He had come to the conclusion that a great and radical change of everything was required and maybe it would come – unfortunately maybe not in the form that anybody wanted.

The Envoy then departed for Japan where his credentials proved unacceptable. In the end it was Viceroy Li Hung Chang who took his place with plenary powers to negotiate a peace

Events took an unexpected turn when just as he arrived to take up his post, a fanatic shot him in the face. The Japanese were so distraught at this breach of diplomatic protocol that their natural chivalrous nature compelled them to grant him more favourable terms than they had at first intended.

14 – A Time for Change

1894

Timothy and his wife had decided that it was necessary for the two younger daughters to be given an English education in the surroundings where they would eventually live. The schooling in Shanghai did not provide such a good standard as could be obtained back home, so Mrs. Richard returned with her two daughters leaving Timothy in Shanghai.

It was not long before he felt that he too needed a change to stimulate his mind and so he left for the adjoining province of Zhejiang. His reason being the desire to learn more about Buddhism.

In May of 1895 he set out with the Rev. Ernest Box for the then famous Buddhist centre of T'ien-t'ai, near Ningpo. Ningpo was once famed for traditional Chinese furniture production. It was from this centre that had sprung the most popular Buddhist sect that had spread throughout China and Japan. Each Buddhist sect based its teaching on one or other of the Buddhist Scriptures, this particular one was founded on the Lotus Scripture, the principal object of worship being Amitabha and Paradise as the abode of the soul after death. Timothy was drawn to it by its remarkable similarity to Christianity mainly its doctrine of "Salvation by Faith" rather than the "Works" of orthodox Buddhism.

A Mr. Tung, a Manchu Christian from Peking, accompanied them. He had been exposed to all the various forms of Christianity having been baptised as Roman Catholic, confirmed in the Greek Church, studied medicine under the Presbyterians and worked under Bishop Scott of the S.P.G. Richard, unsurprisingly thought of him as a very open minded man willing to prove and explore all things and hold on to those that he considered good. His reason for being with them was somewhat odd. Having been exposed to so many variations of Christianity, he had decided that he would visit the Pope and invite him to come to China with the aim of uniting all of the Christian bodies residing there. There was one flaw in his plan – he did not have any money! As was normal for the time he had called on Timothy in the hope that he would be granted some travel expenses. Timothy, having listened to his plans and realising the impracticability of the scheme took Mr. Tung under his wing, wrote to Bishop Scott that he would be not be seeing him for some time and then, to occupy his mind, took him to this Buddhist centre.

This area of China was new to Timothy. The Yangtse basically divided China north and south. Timothy had mainly travelled the north where it was dry, dusty and then would suddenly become wet and cloggy with transportation mainly by horses, mules, donkeys and carts. What he saw now were mainly buffalo, ox, goat, pigs and dogs, transport was mainly by boat or chair. And so it was by this form of transport that they made their way to Ka-li-zen. During this journey as they passed through some trees, they came across a number of robbers hanging in cages with their feet just off the ground, their guide told them that eventually they would starve to death. Further on they came across some human heads which appeared to have been there for some time hanging in their respective cages – justice was certainly harsh in this area.

Here he found that the people were much more superstitious. A large number of shops trading purely sold clothing for the dead and for erecting facsimile houses for them to lie in. The wealthier made the clothes and houses to the same quality as if they were for living in them. Here paper money was much more in evidence. He watched groups of people in worship. One group were in a shop where four Buddhist pictures 500mm x 150mm had been placed in gilt frames facing the street. Knelt before them were four semi-religious men, not clean-shaven like the priests but wearing their religious vestments. One of them beat a bell so that the rest could keep time as they recited one of the Buddhist Scriptures. Another group were more absorbed in their ceremony and mainly comprised middle aged women surrounding one man – arranging themselves in a horseshoe shape and they too were chanting, in unison the Mito Scripture of the Buddhists. Both groups, evidently, were saying prayers for the sick; as this was the custom in the area rather than send for doctors.

The next scene he came across was at an old memorial arch, about to be repaired having been built to commemorate a man who had supposedly lived to be a hundred.

For two hundred yards either side along the street that ran to the arch, the inhabitants had built straw men to ward off evil spirits. These straw men varied in height from one to five feet tall. Some were also placed on roofs, some had spears, some had bows and arrows and others had rifles, all had been blessed with the task of repelling any attack from evil spirits. Effigies of monkeys and other long tailed animals were also prevalent.

With all this inherent fear of evil influences Timothy saw it as a golden opportunity to expand his missionary work.

He found that certain words were taboo – for fear of harming the silkworms – upon which the majority of the population relied for their income. You could not say "death" but instead use the word "peace"; "tea" suggested snakes so "broth" was used and "oil" evidently conveyed the impression of swimming in the water, which contained innumerable poisonous items, and so "wood" would have to be substituted. During the silkworm season all doors had to remain closed and no visitors were allowed and no one but no one was to talk for fear of the worms getting ill and dying.

After this visit they then transferred to a small boat to reach Hangchow, which was about 110 miles south – west of Shanghai. It had been a very important city in the past having been the capital of the Sung Dynasty and consequently contained many Buddhist temples. Many of these had been destroyed in the Tai-ping uprising but were now under construction again. Surprisingly they found a Buddhist bookshop and procured several items the most useful being a guide to all the temples around them. One temple they were recommended to visit was Lin-Ying Sz that was some three miles to the west of the

West Lake. The approach to the temple was beautifully laid out. You entered through an avenue of trees with the figures of Buddha and his followers carved into a huge limestone rock to one side, then you came to the gigantic Heavenly Guardians about twenty feet tall after that. These have since been destroyed by various rebels, however by passing through a barely visible entrance into the western court of the temple there was another sight to marvel – five hundred, larger than life size, gilded figures, each one different and each one representing a disciple of Buddha. The priests were going around lighting incense and placing it in front of each figure. This filled the whole temple with a rich aromatic smoke.

Their next visit was to another temple towards the east of the city – this was called Hai-chao-Sz [Sz being the word for temple] and this was the main monastery in Hangchow where any priest passing had the right to stay free of charge, all told there were about twenty of these establishments around Hangchow. In this temple three divinities were worshipped and these figures were sat on a platform some twenty feet high and they themselves were an additional ten feet high.

They now set off for the holy mountain about 160 miles away stopping at Shao-hsien at about one third distance. This city was well known for its wines and its lawyers, whether the two were linked it is not known but every one of the magistrates serving in China had to have an advisor who had to come from this area. The wine was made from rice and was exported all over China in earthenware jars and was usually served slightly warm. Distilleries were not very widespread as the process of producing distilled spirits had not arrived until the Mongol Dynasty of 1260-1368 and then was kept secret from the masses. This area had been under the influence of French control until the revolution. The buildings were mostly stone and the main crop grown was rice in the paddy fields consequently most of the journey was done by boat. Hiring was easy. You bought one ticket for the whole of your trip and you stopped at stations en route either to embark onto a fresh boat or to transfer onto a chair if the geography changed. Each coolie was paid a fixed daily rate.

The time soon came when they had to transfer to another boat to travel between Shao-hsien and Ching-hsien, this time it was rowed by three men. The land here is flat and subject to many floods in the rainy season. It is also studded with little towns all linked by canals, which go to the foot of the mountains at the edge of the plain. The river here was tidal and hard to navigate with a strong current running against them. With the shallow water they were compelled to tow the boat from the bank and then when it grounded to wade waist deep into the water and push it along. They now had four boatmen but still only managed to make fifteen miles in a day. The next day was even harder as they had to navigate rocks in the strong current and grounded the boat several times. Here they observed the farmers growing the rice crop. When the land was flooded they would plough with the help of water buffalo, it was then harrowed under water. The farmer then collected from a bed plants that he had allowed to grow about four inches above the water and plucking them up into small bundles as thick as an arm, tied them and then threw them around the area he has just harrowed. Tucking his trousers up he then took one bundle at a time and he separated about ten sprouts and planted them in the muddy water about ten inches apart in rows about a foot apart. It would only take about three days for these to take root and grow. The farmer then returned and this time on his knees stirred up the mud around the roots with his fingers thus causing the plant to grow more quickly.

The boat journey now took them past Shin-ching-hsein where they went to see the largest image of Buddha in China. It was cut out of the rock in a sitting posture and above it was a temple carved out of the same cliff with over a thousand smaller Buddha images contained within.

They finally reached T'ien-t'ai. On the mountain he could see that there were temples and monasteries every three or four miles apart. They passed through the three most important temples in the area, the first Ching-Liang was about 1,580 feet above sea level, twelve miles further on was Ti-Tsang temple at 2,750 feet a further five miles and they reached Wan Nien at 2,400 feet. Here the chief hall was in the centre with two minor ones to the east and west. On the first floor was an image of Vairochama, an ancient god above which was a red ball, said to represent the light emanating from him. The adjacent hall had five galleries of images about fifteen inches high, three sides of the hall had large transparent doors and above this in a loft was the library of Buddhist Scriptures. Timothy saw that not all of the shelves were full and some of the contents had been torn and gnawed by rats. Then they were summoned to observe a service, which started with a bell ringing, and the rhythm of a drum broke out. With the bell, triangle and the beating of a wooden dish they started to sing – all choosing a different note- and then ending it with them all chanting in unison.

The next day, having spent the night in the temple, they travelled five miles to the Shining Light temple. Here lived six chief abbots on the mountain with ages ranging from thirty-seven to seventy. There were a total of seventy-two temples and over a hundred hermits huts. Most were now in ruin. As they were so near they went to see one of the hermits. He was locked up in his room receiving his food through a fifteen-inch diameter hole in the wall. This hermit had come from Shanghai and had vowed to live this existence for four years to free his mind of evil thoughts. He had no objection to being photographed and posed with his head peering out through the hole. They then passed on to the highest temple at 3,400 feet where they eat with the abbot and then ventured on to the peak at over 4,000 feet. There due to the mist, they could not take any more pictures. Coming back down they took the opportunity to visit several more hermits' huts. The first one they came to nobody answered when they knocked on the door. The next one contained a man with his head completely shaven. He was sat cross-legged on a chair reading a religious book. Timothy totally surprised him by conversing in his own tongue and then displaying his knowledge by asking if he understood the prophecy contained in the sixth chapter where it said " Five hundred years after me there will come the Fountain of all the Buddhas". The hermits' attitude immediately changed, here was a foreigner who had some understanding of other faiths. He asked if they would like some tea and then enquired if Timothy himself understood the meaning of the prophecy. Timothy explained that as far as he was concerned it was a prophecy of Jesus Christ, who appeared five hundred years after Buddha. The hermit replied that he had never had the passage interpreted before, although he had been reading for some thirty years. After thanking him for his hospitality they went to the next hut where there lived a man and wife both around seventy years old. They earned their living by picking tea, which they sold on. Pointing to a sealed door with a hole of about a foot diameter, Timothy asked if there was a priest on the other side, the wife confirmed that there was but he should not be disturbed as he was carrying out his prayers and meditation. The abbot told them that there were just over a hundred people living in the huts dotted around the area and that they never ever appeared unless the person concerned had given a charitable donation to the monastery. Moving on they came to another temple where one of the monks came out to greet them as he had heard that Timothy was on his way down and had met him once before in Shanghai. He told them that the abbot there had collected over 13,000 dollars to rebuild the monastery. Going on down they passed further temples and came across more Buddhist libraries and then a vast eating area where there stood large rice pots some seven feet in diameter. These were used to feed the 160 priests who belonged to the place and who were now seated on cushions placed on a wooden bench that ran around the wall of the Meditation Hall. At midday they witnessed a large gathering of women, all over forty years old, moving into the yards of the various compounds. Evidently they had assembled to "beg for a dream" a custom in that region. Should they have a dream that night then they had to go to a friend – not a priest- for them to interpret what it meant. If the friend told them that it was a dream that would bring them happiness or good fortune, they would return to the temple to either burn incense or offer prayers.

During that evening they were having supper with the priest when the babble of women talking grew ever louder. Timothy asked if he could see what was going on. The priest replied that it was no problem and carrying a lamp escorted them to the court of the True Prince. Being the twelfth night of the moon the sky was bright and light and framed in the middle of the hall by about a dozen red candles was the idol that the women worshipped. On the floor, they saw the about a hundred women lying down, fully clothed but with no bedding, on one side of the room, seated at a table, were about half a dozen men reading prayer books. The leader appeared to be much older. Looking around they saw that women were also lying down outside the temple, on the veranda and in the courtyard. A couple of priests moved amongst them making sure that all was in order whilst the majority of the other priests settled down in other courtyards. Returning to their rooms they heard the sound of music, which lasted for about an hour, and then all went quiet.

They were woken the following morning by the loud ringing of bells. It was about three in the morning and together with the drum beats that were now booming they saw that the priests were reciting their prayers. In the hall of the True Prince about five women were going through the same process with two elderly men leading them. Timothy then came across a man who was reciting a Buddhist prayer so fast that he had to stop to get his breath. He did this so mechanically and repeatedly that he was able to listen to what Timothy was saying and count his beads at the same time!

Leaving the temple they passed the remains of phallic worship some two feet high placed in grounds of a small garden. Here their priest guide stopped and pointing out their route back to Shanghai wished them well on their journey.

As they progressed, one thing struck them. There were hardly any animals either carrying goods or carts. All of this work appeared to be undertaken by men. Generally overloaded they struggled along the pitted roads. The only beasts they saw were water buffaloes, used for ploughing and cows. Hardly a horse was to be seen anywhere. That night they rested in an inn and hanging on a wall was a large paper banner with the following written on it :-

A Fine Tonic Prescription for Mankind
Called "The Tincture of Purity"

Yin Yang	The whole
Favours	Enough
Careful speech	To flavour
Straightforwardness	Three grains
Duty	According to the occasion
Love and righteousness	Practise extensively
Honesty	One piece
Goodness of heart	A slice
Carefulness	A bit

Gambling	Wash entirely away
Faith	Be careful of
Peace-making	A lump
Joy	A large quantity
Bowels of mercy	The whole length
Patience	10,000 parts
Worship of heaven and earth	A pure heart
As much as needed	Days and months

They were soon taken to a room that was below the level of the road where they were motioned to sit. A short while later a young girl came in and ushered them upstairs to another room. This time they found themselves level with the road to the rear of the inn. On the floor were strips of straw, about 3 inches thick and sewn together to form a mattress. Each was rolled up so that it formed a pillow allowing you to sleep in whatever direction you chose. Evidently it was common for two to sleep head to tail when the inn was busy. These mattresses were spread all along the floor and that night there were sixteen of them sleeping in that one room. Lying down and looking up Timothy could see that there were boards suspended from the ceiling like wooden hammocks where about six more people could be accommodated if required.

They stayed a month in Hang Chow, the weather for a change was perfect and the countryside beautiful. The canals were much larger in this region, about four or five times as wide as those further north around Peking. In contrast to the barren countryside that they had just come from, all was lush and green with fruit trees in profusion and many flowers he had not seen before. There were many islands generally with a high sycamore clump in the centre and surrounded by plum trees or ash and at the waters edge were the mulberry trees for the silk worms which he watched being fed. In the distance they could see the snow capped mountain ranges.

They went to one market and found nearly all the objects for sale were made of paper such as silver and gold shoes, rolls of dollars with one hundred bills in each roll, paper models of houses, horses men and women. All of these destined to be burnt at funerals. Stacked outside shops that usually fronted timber yards were rows of coffins all of various grades and prices. Some highly polished with gold inlays for the very rich down to rough-hewn shells for the poor. Bodies could remain unburied for months or years whilst the geomancers made their decisions about the correct place and date.

And so the time came for them to once more return to Shangai.

15 – A Time of Revolution

In 1895 anti foreigner & missionary fervour was mounting. Eleven missionaries, mostly women, were massacred in the province of Fukien. [Fujian] Many years previous, Timothy had sat on a committee that had intended to present a memorial to the Throne in memory of those persecuted for their beliefs. Due to other more pressing commitments the progress was delayed and this incident now acted as a catalyst. Timothy found himself being recalled and deputed to go to Peking to take any action as was found necessary. In Peking he was to consult with two resident Drs. – Wherry and Blodget. A shorter and more practical memorial signed by twenty leading missionaries and several Bishops was drawn up and Timothy made his way to the capital city. On arrival he found that Blodgett had gone on holiday. With Wherry he had the hand written memorial carefully bound into a book and through the auspices of an American foreign advisor contacted the ex-viceroy Li, who still exercised considerable influence. His objective was to gain access to Prince Kung, President of the Yamen. The advisor, a Mr. Pethick, insisted on an audience with Li, as he knew that Li wanted to meet him again. The Viceroy was pleased to see them both and insisted that they sat down to dinner with him.

The conversation that followed was very revealing. From the discussion they had during the meal they learnt that: -

A] The Emperor was incapable of making up his own mind, he was entirely dependant on advisors.

B] That the greater majority of influential mandarins new nothing about foreign matters.

C] That he felt that all those around him were plotting against him.

D] That the high ministers in Peking regarded Western education as the work of the devil.

E] That the essays that were in the minds of those who sat exams were of no practical use.

F] That the number of those capable of intellectual thought was very small.

After this interview Pethick told Timothy that the Prime Minister, Weng T'ung Ho, was in all but name the Emperor of China and that the government gave scant regard to any treaties and consequently those in the Chinese civil service often complained about the amount of pressure put on them by foreign ministers in Peking. He also told Timothy that it would be beneficial if he could use Prime Minister Weng to obtain an introduction to Prince Kung so that he could make his own observations to back up what he just been told.

Timothy later on decided to ask Viceroy Li if there was any possibility of sending a hundred academics [Hanlins] abroad and arranging a syllabus for teaching some members of the Imperial Clan on foreign affairs. He pointed out that whilst they were paying Japan two hundred million taels per annum to buy peace, they could generate twice that amount by exploiting their own natural resources. Li told Timothy that all of this was playing with fire, no official would be brave enough promote these thoughts and besides, the anti foreigner spirit prevailed in all of the highest posts in the Cabinet, in fact Hu Tung, the head of the cabinet, was even accused of treasonable acts by talking to foreign diplomats. It was clear to him that whilst the anti-foreigner feelings prevailed amongst these old men of government the Hanlins and reformers were helpless, they could not even count on the support of the Manchus.

Li suggested that he sent all of his books to Prince Kung and that he would advise him on how to couch his letter in terms that were acceptable so that they at least had a chance of getting past Weng. A few days later Timothy took his idea of how he thought the letter should look to Li who immediately re-drafted it. Handing it back to Timothy he advised that on his introduction to Weng, he should start off by praising him over and above anything that he deserved and then afterwards start sticking whatever knives he wanted into his back. Li also said that paradoxically Prince Kung was as hard as stone whilst his Prime Minister could be worked very easily especially if sated with platitudes.

It took until October for his appointment to arrive to see Weng and on leaving for Shanghai he wrote to his wife about his feelings.

"I feel nervous about going to Peking on such a mighty errand, to try and help to change the mind of a quarter of the human race from a course set for millenniums to a better one in regard to the world at large."

He was now beginning to feel the strain of his responsibilities and suffered from frequent bouts of neuralgia. Writing again to his wife:

"At the most exciting times I could only sleep in a very fragmented way, getting up [as you know] ever so many times to write down some fresh ideas. Often too, in the early morning, before getting up, I would get fresh thoughts that would fully occupy me during the day. They were like clear orders and it was a delight to obey them."

The long awaited interview with Weng took place on the 26th of October. As with all formal interviews in those days it started off in the presence of a swarm of underlings. After a while Weng took Timothy into a private room accompanied only by his right-hand man Wang Ming Luan. There Timothy presented his evidence of the persecution of missionaries and Christians and clearly stated that as far as he was concerned all of this was done with the permission of the Government – he took with him two books written by the Chinese that claimed and described what Christians were capable of doing to the Chinese.

"The first book, by Wei, stated that Christians scooped out the eyes of the Chinese and mixed them up with lead to produce silver. The other book stated that missionaries made bewitching medicine that demented women, and produced photographs that stole away the soul of those photographed. I pointed out to the Prime Minister that these false and defamatory statements were made in order to damage the reputation of Christians and were pure invention to create anti-Christian riots. He asked me who were the miscreants responsible, and I replied they were Chinese officials. He remarked that could not possibly be true. In reply, I took up one of the bundles, opened it at the place where the false charges were made, and then showed the Preface to the first volume by Tso T'sung-t'tang, the great Viceroy who had won back Ili from the Russians, and said: " You must know that this man was an eminent official." Then I took the other bundle, folded the page containing the false accusations, and turning to the first volume, showed that it was inscribed with name of Wang Wen-shao, Viceroy of Yunnan and Kweichow. " You will know that this man is also a High Chinese official and I added : " You must be well aware that these books have lately been republished, like the Blue Books of China in a cheap form for wide distribution throughout the Empire. When the ordinary people read these defamations, published in a popular form, with the names and sanction of the highest officials in the land, we cannot wonder that they are incited to stir up riots and massacre the Christians."

"Seeing I had proved my point up to the hilt, the Prime Minister replied, laughing, "You have lived too long in China," and he gave up questioning my statements.

"After this, I pointed out how China had been troubled with religious difficulties for a thousand years before; first the Buddhists had persecuted the Taoists, then the Taoists persecuted the Buddhists and consequently there was no peace. Once religious liberty had been granted, peace and quiet reigned throughout the land. All I ask from the Government is that we Christians be let alone."

The Prime Minister was astounded at the simplicity of the request stating "If that is all I can easily promise it". He also asked Timothy to prepare a statement on what he considered to be needful reforms for China at that juncture.

The Prime Minister told Timothy that as far as he was concerned he was a just and fair man and that in fact he had heard those comments made by others before he had met him. Li now told Timothy to send his book to Prince Kung and actually revised his draft letter to request an interview, a letter of introduction was not required as Timothy's name was now very well known in Court circles.

Timothy wrote in his diary "Prince Kung was the brother of the late Emperor Hsien Feng, and was the Manchu Plenipotentiary who had saved the situation in 1860-1861. He was the most imperious man I ever met, every inch a prince, with a demeanour as if he felt himself a god among men. It was said he was the only man in the Empire of whom the Empress Dowager was afraid. They had many stormy times, and she often found it expedient to bend her will to his."

Timothy received notification of his appointment to see Prince Kung on October 30th. The venue was to be the Tsungli Yamen and since he was attending so had all seven members of the Yamen. To put Timothy in his place he sat him next to the door, a sign that he did not hold him in very high regard, it did not bode well when he opened the interview by referring to all Christians as the scum of the earth. He said it should be taken for granted that all the troubles brought upon the Christians were of their own making by being disloyal to China and inherently foolish in their actions. Having let him give vent to his views Timothy asked if he might be given the opportunity to express his views on the subject. Kung duly granted him the time to do so.

Timothy stated that the charges that Prince Kung quoted against the Christians simply were not true and the Government's actions based on these self same charges were unjust. He pointed out that he had spent many years in several different provinces of China seeing the good that the different Christian societies had done and knew the reality of what was going on, whilst he, Prince Kung, had mainly spent his life within the confines of Peking getting his information by hearsay and mostly from those that had a particular axe to grind. Timothy made plain that he had not come in any private capacity nor as an ambassador of any country but as a representative of all Protestant Christians of the world. He challenged Kung to set up a Commission of Inquiry into all of the alleged charges he had heard stating that if found guilty of any crimes they would not avoid just punishment but if they were innocent he was sure that the Prince would see that in turn justice would be done to them by granting them the same liberty as extended to other religions in China.

It was a powerful speech and afterwards one of the Emperor's tutors, a high member of the Yamen came across and thanked Timothy for speaking frankly and in a manner that no one there would dare do. He congratulated him on putting his request in such a way that he still showed respect so that no offence could be taken.

Several of the bystanders also came up to Timothy and thanked him for translating Mackensies's *Nineteenth Century* which he had done in 1893 and they told him that it was now widely read. Timothy told them that he recalled hearing about a Russian minister who had an interview with Prince Kung some time back and had asked him if he had read the translation. Kung replied that he had and when asked what he thought of it replied that it was a very useful book for China. The minister, Count Cassini, told Kung "Then I am afraid that you have not grasped the moral of it – it teaches democracy versus autocracy. If those views were to become current throughout China then you – 6,000,000 Manchus will be outvoted by the remaining 400,000,000 of Chinese and you will be gone!"

This prophecy was to come true in the revolution of 1911.

Viceroy Li now busied himself drafting introductions for Timothy and Dr. Wherry to go to the Foreign Office. British German and American ministers were also approached and the Missionary Memorial explained to them. The Germans declined to co-operate but the British and American delegations decided to proceed.

The gist of the Memorial was basically that:-

Although the Chinese Government allowed freedom for the Confucian, Buddhist, Taoist and Mohammedan religions to practice for a thousand years, ever since

Emperor Yung Ching in the 1700's Christians had been continually persecuted even though several treaties had been made offering protection. The Government had published propaganda in the form of official reports in which they detailed gruesome and horrific practices carried out by Christians that were patently untrue. The result of this meant that officials and scholars believed them to be true as they were published with the full consent of the highest Viceroys and consequently encouraged the populace to carry out persecutions, attacks and riots. All of this resulted in burning chapels, killing their own people and foreign missionaries and their families. It ended by stating that not only had western civilisation benefited from Christianity, but so had the inhabitants of all the continents and small islands – the adoption of Western civilization by Japan had propelled it forward and this had been done mainly through the influence of the missionary movement.

It also pointed out the good work done in translating the Sacred Books of China and its history into Western languages and had had a major input into famine relief in Shantung, Shansi, Kiangsu and Manchuria. What the missionaries desired was for the Chinese Government to learn from their example and to link in to their international knowledge to help avoid further tensions within the country.

Timothy ended by requesting that Christians be left alone to carry out their good work and prayed that an edict would be announced granting these requests.

A few days later, the Prince instructed the Chinese Foreign Office to enter into dialogue with missionaries until the matter was resolved to the satisfaction of all parties. All was going smoothly and an edict was expected within days when suddenly one of the strongest supporters in the Chinese delegation was demoted. This weakened the pro Memorial bargaining position and then out of the blue the French minister objected to the Throne granting any form of missionary request as it meant that they could deal directly with the Chinese Government, the French for a long time had harboured a secret desire to be the main communication channel to the Throne. Timothy was now called to give a brief to the British and American Legations on how far their discussions with the Yamen had got and how much influence the French minister had. This intervention by the French meant that an edict would not be issued but Timothy was somewhat heartened to hear that there would not be any more anti-Christian literature issued and that all local authorities had been instructed to behave in a more positive manner towards the missionaries.

16 – The Start of Change

There was in China, at this time, a noted Cantonese scholar called K'ang Yu-wei, a Doctor of Literature. Many regarded him as a modern sage. He had written copious works countering the traditional thoughts of the Chinese. He was so influential in certain circles that the government felt compelled to try to challenge some of his outpourings even to the extent of destroying some of his works and the printing blocks from which they were produced. He was however as anti-foreign as anyone in China. Clad in bright yellow silk, he went to see Timothy when he was in Peking in October 1895. Explaining that he was leaving the following day for the south, he had brought some of his books en route as a present and on meeting Timothy spoke to him saying-

" Coming down to Hong- Kong from Canton on my way to Peking for my degree, I was struck by the sense of order in the place with its wide streets and evident cleanliness. Prior to this I had been told that the area had been occupied by so called barbarians and I found that they were not barbarians after all but highly civilised and gentle folk, with whom it was a pleasure to engage in conversation. On entering Shanghai my new conception was reinforced and I began to realise that maybe outside China there could well be a civilisation superior to our own. When I got to Peking and saw the state and condition of our capital, I was disgusted; for, instead of finding the Celestial Capital which in my dreams should have been ahead of these ports, I found that they were far behind them. It was then that I decided to study Western literature."

He intimated that he wanted to co-operate with Timothy in the work of regenerating China. This was a scoop indeed!

K'ang was now at war with the traditionalists. He devoured as much western literature as he could get his hands on. He then drew up a memorandum much on the basis as recommended by the S.D.K publications and implored the Emperor to enter into discussion with Timothy and take immediate steps to reform China and try to drag it into the modern world. Such was K'ang's influence that this memorandum was speedily signed by a further 10,000 scholars. A Junior Reform society was established in Shanghai with branches in other cities. They brought their draft of the rules that they wanted to apply to Timothy to revise and discussed with him the methods that they should apply to bring about the enlightenment of their country.

It was not long after that Timothy was asked to read K'ang's memorandum to the Emperor and was astounded to find that all the various suggestions that he [Timothy] had made had been boiled down to one clear and succinct statement. However he did notice that it was still very parochial with little or no international or universal context.

Bolstered by these radical younger Chinese, the Reform Society grew rapidly, primarily amongst the Hanlin or Academicians but also with members from the censors and under-secretaries of the Grand Council – this was potentially dangerous as it was never clear which way their support would go or who were their true masters. For 700 years the Peking Gazette had been the sole official publication for memorials, decrees and appointments. Now there was there was a new independent publication backed by secret subscription and issued by the Reform party. It adopted the somewhat long title of *Wan Kuo Kung Pao,* exactly the same title as that of the S.D.K.'s Review of the Times. At first it used reprints of this magazine but as the S.D.K. publication was printed from metallic type the Reform version was printed from wooden type as used in the official Government organ so that outwardly it had every appearance of being of being from a legitimate source whilst its contents promoted Western ideas.

Timothy at this time desperately required a temporary secretary whilst he stayed in Peking and was lucky enough to be offered the services of Liang Ch'I-ch'ao, who later became one of the most prolific "modern" Chinese writers of his time. He had around him many of those with access to the Imperial Court and Governors although one of them, the son of the Governor of Hupeh, would be beheaded within two years in a failed Coup d'etat. Dangerous times indeed. Opposition was being stoked up by those who were challenging its ideals and although the Reformers were desperate for Timothy to change his plans and stay in Peking he could not fight the might of the Government, led by the father in law of Lord Li's son. So the doors of the Reform Society were closed and pasted up. Later Viceroy Li was to deny any knowledge or connection with this act to Timothy and arranged for a grant to be made of 12,000 taels a year as some form of reparation and arranged for him to see the Prime Minister. This resulted in Timothy being asked to write a brief on Reform and the implications of its adoption.

"After prefacing that God showed no partiality towards any nation, East or West, that the nation that obeyed Heaven prospered and the nation that disobeyed perished, according to unalterable law, I pointed out four vital requirements for China : educational reform, economic reform, internal and international peace, and spiritual regeneration.

To carry out these great measures I proposed:

1. Two foreign advisors to the Throne

2. A Cabinet of eight ministers, one half of Manchus and Chinese and the other half of foreign officials who would know about the progress of all of the world.

3. The immediate reform of currency and the establishment of finance on a sound basis.

4. The immediate building of railways and the opening of mines and factories.

5. The establishment of a Board of Education to introduce modern schools and colleges throughout the Empire.

6. The establishment of an intelligent Press with experienced foreign journalists to assist Chinese editors for the enlightenment of the people.

7.   The building up of an adequate army and navy for
       the country's defence

Timothy was now in driving seat with the potential to
change the way that China was governed and how it faced
off to the rest of the world.

This visionary scheme, far reaching and daring
incorporated many of Timothy's previously held beliefs
and parts of them he had submitted to high officials before
only to see them put away for "future consideration"

This time it was actually shown to the Emperor who
having asked who was the originator subsequently gave
his approval to initiate the proposed actions.

Timothy then entered into correspondence to put some
meat on the proposals recommending Sir Robert Hart and
Sir Charles Addis and two Americans, a Mr Foster and
Commissioner Drew to serve on the Board. The Prime
Minister however had other ideas and thought that it
would only require one able foreigner to be in charge
and suggested to Timothy that he should be that man.
This was not what Timothy wanted and as he pointed out
how was he to do the work of four men, besides he had
no wish to become a member of the Chinese civil service
and more importantly it would take him away from his
missionary work.

On the 12th of October he was asked if he would have a
talk with Sun Chia-nai, the Emperor's "tutor" or personal
advisor. On hearing this, Viceroy Li advised Timothy to
speak to the tutor as if he actually was the Emperor as he
was the real power behind the throne. On meeting Chia
–nai, he found him to be a very cultured and courteous

man of about sixty years. He learnt that together, he and the Emperor had read Timothy's *History* over a two month period. The Empress Dowager had now relinquished her control on government and had taken up residence in the Summer Palace. It was not lost on Timothy that ironically this beautiful building stacked full of ancient Chinese art had been burnt down by the British in retaliation for the barbaric treatment of British subjects in 1860. Funds were then diverted by the Chinese government to rebuild the palace to its former glory, funds that originally were destined for the modernisation of the navy. The consequence of this act was the easy defeat of the Chinese by the Japanese in 1894.

Timothy decided that rather than enter into discussions on his leading the Reform Board, he would let matters progress at a pace that suited the Chinese and so he decided to leave Peking only to find that he was then being offered the post of President in the soon to be formed Peking University. Once more declining yet another post he was offered the same post in Shanghai University declining yet again but this time recommending a friend –Dr. John Fryer- for the post.

Later, on his way to England he received a third invitation to serve within the Government; but replied that he could do better work for China as an independent rather than as a servant. It would appear that the Chinese authorities were desperate to tap into his unique knowledge and ability to network with foreign diplomats.

The next crisis he had to resolve came later that year when he was summonsed to Peking to see the former Chinese minister to America, Chang Yin-hwan. He was told that plans for a rebellion had been found in the possession of a man called Sun who had taken shelter in a Christian chapel in Canton. This was obviously a major problem, as this man having sought refuge with Christians put a spoke in any chance of settlement of the missionary question, a major plank in Timothy's reform agenda.

His answer to this was to state that surely this was an isolated incident and was of considerably less importance than the Confucianist rebellions over the ages. Chang found this response extremely amusing and congratulated him on his grasp of Chinese intellect stating that Prince Kung was now in poor health and that the Prime Minister was totally ignorant of foreign affairs since he was being guided by the censors of whom he lived in total fear, this left only Viceroy Li and himself with any knowledge of such things and consequently all foreign issues devolved on him. Clearly Timothy felt that he had been given a covert message as to whom he should deal with in the future.

The next person he sat down to talk with was one he had last met in the 1880's then as Governor of Shansi, Councillor Kang Yi. When he saw him then he was an obstinate man always vetoing any proposal for improvement. Ki was a Manchu and would soon start his reactionary practices again, only this time they would have far more serious consequences, as he was one of the catalysts for the Boxer troubles in Peking. Ki was heavily influenced by astrology having spent many nights, while in Shansi, studying the stars and reading into them their effect and influence on personal and national destiny.

Surprisingly, at this meeting Timothy found him to be extremely friendly. From this easy going discussion he found that Kang's Manchu background came with considerable baggage and that the gulf between them and the Chinese was constantly simmering with jealousy. Timothy desperately tried to impress on him that the only way forward was to study and embrace the good points of other nations and asked if it would be at all possible for the Empress Dowager to invite two foreign ladies to act as palace tutors on the ways of the wider world and two further tutors be supplied for his Majesty, could he even have a discussion with the Emperor himself?

The next day a messenger arrived to say that Kang had little or no influence with the Emperor as he was guided by the all powerful Prime Minister who ensured that in the Cabinet the Chinese held sway and carried the vote on all matters.

Imagine his surprise when, as he was preparing to go to Peking, a card was delivered to his room at the London Mission building. Thinking that this was a formal courtesy and that he ought to reply with own card in the same vein, he was totally surprised to be told that the Prime Minister was actually outside and wanted to see him now. This was unprecedented. Here was the man who he had been told was the real powerhouse in Chinese politics, asking to see him!

They talked for more than an hour on religious tolerance and political reform, during which the Prime Minister apologised for the non-publication of the missionary edict, saying that this was due to fact that none of his colleagues would support him. Timothy begged that he try to treat all people – Christians and non-Christians – as possessing equal rights. The Prime Minister responded that it would be helpful if Timothy could help to resuscitate the Reform Club. Timothy was wary. Once again he was in danger of being caught up in political affairs and suggested that he be approached later when the club could be guaranteed and seen to be a real force for serving China and not a centre for intrigue.

They parted on good terms with Prime Minister honouring him with several rolls of silk and two rare dark blue and gold vases.

At last he now was now ready for a long break.

17 – Home Again

Timothy had now been in China for over twenty six years and felt that he owed it to himself and his family to return home and reflect on his future. He had already decided that he needed to publicise the needs of China and the S.D.K. to those in high office back home.

He sailed from Shanghai in a French mail steamer accompanied by four Jesuit priests and a Rev. Shorrock of Shensi Baptist Missionary Society all travelling second class and since none could speak each others language they conversed in Chinese. By coincidence Viceroy Li was also on board – travelling first class, as were his secretaries- to the coronation of the Tsar. Li expressed surprise that man of Timothy's importance should be travelling in such restrained circumstances to which Timothy cheekily replied that he did not have the obvious wealth that the Chinese Government had and could throw at *some* of its citizens.

They stopped off at India visiting another friend in Madras who took them on a tour of the local schools. Having been warned not to travel across India during May, as cholera was rampant, they nevertheless took the risk and boarded a small steamer for Calcutta, where Shorrock succumbed to the disease narrowly escaping death. They then left by evening train for Benares [Varanasi] but somehow managed to get off at the wrong station. They rode thro' the streets in a gharry, a form of horse drawn cab, the excessive heat almost overcoming them – it was far hotter than anything they had experienced in China. On arrival at the correct destination the hostess was totally amazed that they had even attempted to travel in the heat and further more "did they not notice that there was hardly anyone else outside?" She immediately sent them to bed to cool down until the evening and called for the punkah-wallahs to operate the bed punkahs. Next day they were refreshed and went around Benares seeing the bathers in the Ganges and witnessing the cremation ceremonies on the riverbanks. After passing through a few temples they went on to Agra to view the Taj Mahal. To Timothy he was more impressed when they saw the Kutab Minar at Delhi. To him it was like a model telescope up which they could ascend and watch the sunrise. This and the Kutab had been built by the Moslem rulers of India and in the centre of the Mosque's courtyard was an ancient iron pillar supposedly erected several hundred years before Christ.

Back in Bombay the heat was still oppressive, with a vast number of its inhabitants sleeping on the pavements as even they could not stand the heat inside their houses. Next day when embarking on the French mail steamer, even he almost fainted. He was glad when they approached the Red Sea where putting on a heavier coat to keep warm seemed bliss. Eventually the boat reached Marseilles that heaving port of all nationalities where Africa entered Europe and where gangs ruled the city. Glad to be on his way he caught the train to Paris where at last his wife and four daughters, the eldest of which he had not seen for ten years joined him. It may be surprising to learn that all the daughters were now schooled at Paris and were fluent in French. After a few weeks the girls were to be sent to Hanover to improve their knowledge of German. On the journey to the station they were lucky not become caught in a whirlwind which passed down an adjacent track and into the main street overturning carriages and buses – killing and maiming several people. Having seen his daughters safely on their way he then returned with his wife to England to see some old friends and members of the Baptist Missionary Society. Here he showed them all the books and literature he had produced in China, from the New Testament that he had given to the Empress Dowager to the leaflets he distributed to those who could read in the Chinese heartland. Of particular interest to his friends were the Chinese pirated copies of his handiwork in the provinces.

Timothy explained that there was a pent up demand in China for knowledge and at the moment it was being supplied mainly by the Japanese, who were publishing their enlightening literature from an agnostic or anti-Christian viewpoint. He felt that whilst China was in the process of cultural change with a strong wish for change from the masses it was important that the west had the ability to publish and distribute its point of view and religious beliefs. He proposed that each Baptist Society allocated one man to join him and that they should have a mission statement -"Conversion by the Million"- and field a team to carry out this programme. Such was his influence that all the Societies agreed to his terms.

He then went further and approached the bible societies to simplify the information they were planning to distribute and make it more explanatory rather than wholesale copies of the scriptures which the average reader found difficult to assimilate, "How do you expect a Chinese person to understand who or what a Pharisee is, or where to find Galilee". This was not met with the unequivocal acceptance. Only the Scottish Bible Society understood his argument about adding more information. Others loftily stated that all they were there to do was to issue *The Book,* others were around to actually explain it! He then with his wife spent their remaining time during 1897, drumming up financial support for S.D.K. before setting off for China via Canada, where they drummed up further support for their cause.

18 – China and the Reform Movement

Whilst Timothy had been away the Reform movement had spread rapidly through the country. His friend Dr Allen who was still working on publications printed by the S.D.K. had not appreciated the extent, eagerness or the effect that each issue had on the general population. His *History of the War* –the Chino-Japanese War, had been so influential in the upper streams of government, that he had been invited to head the new university about to be established in Shanghai. Declining, instead he drew up a System for National Education, based on the system that the British Government had introduced into India. Liang, Timothy's secretary, had in the meantime, started a newspaper in Shanghai called *Chinese Progress* in which he urged the educated classes to adopt the ideas of the Reform Movement. This crusade was backed by a masterstroke on his part. Instead of using the high form of language beloved and only understood by advanced scholars, he adopted a more widely understood form – basically, the language of the people but more erudite so that even scholars came to admire it as an ideal form of communication. So successful was this form of communication, that even the bitterly anti-foreign province of Hunan changed its outlook and invited Liang to become president of a Reform College in its capital. With the Reform movement being taken up by many Chinese, especially the educated classes it spread like wildfire. Missionary conferences were now being held where previously there had been hardly any Chinese attendance and now two thirds of the audience were Chinese. Gradually the barriers of disdain and hatred were being broken down and the edict that variety was the spice of life, even in religion, was being realised.

The Reformers in China now recognised that the old hatred of all foreigners just for the sake of it was not a healthy attitude. China and the Chinese were missing out on the rapid progress that the West had achieved. This even fed down to the long held principle that women had little value in society and now this attitude too was gradually weakening. Until 1897 for instance, there had not been any schools for girls in Shanghai and the education levels of females was very much below that of males. This was one of the barriers that the mission schools succeeded in breaking down so that in 1897 the first purely Chinese school for girls was opened in Shanghai funded by a group of reformers who had turned to Timothy and his wife for advice. They both suggested that they should lead by example and have one of the missionary's daughters as the foreign mistress and that the Chinese were to select one of their daughters as head. Timothy's wife was to be the school's inspector – a post she held up to her death.

Meanwhile in the background, all was not well. Trouble was fermenting. Whilst reform was being championed by the educated elite it was possibly being pushed too far too fast. The traditionalist diehards rose up against K'ang Yu-wei who was spearheading the reform. Timothy was now trying to get him to slow down the pace of change.

He could see that the reform movement would be viewed as a "foreign" implant and if it went off track could bring down not K'ang but the Emperor himself.

In 1898 K'ang, was now secretary of the Foreign Office. The young Emperor became heavily influenced by K'ang and by Chang Yin – Hwan a senior member of the Grand Council, who had represented the Emperor at Queen Victoria's Diamond Jubilee in 1897 who, together with many under secretaries, Viceroys and the literati threw in their lot with the Reform Party who in turn were now desperately looking for a leader.

They rushed out a series of edicts which basically meant that they would abolish the education system that had been in place for over five hundred years, would establish a western type University in Peking for the study of western culture, convert several temples into schools for Western education, establish a translation unit specifically for translating Western learning into Chinese, establish a patent office to encourage lateral thinking and to reverse the flow of new ideas, protect Christianity and to make the Reform paper – *Chinese Progress* – the official organ of the Government, to abolish all inefficient and useless offices in the main cities and provinces, and finally to send young Manchus abroad to study foreign languages.

Timothy was now taking a September break in a seaside resort called Pet t'ai-ho some 200 miles from Peking that had been built by foreigners for their relaxation "western style". There he met Sir Robert Hart who having taken his first holiday in sixteen years, wanted to show him the edicts that had just reached him and which he could hardly believe had been made. "I never expected to live to see this" he exclaimed.

Two weeks later all had changed again, the Empress Dowager had swept back into power and issued a new set of edicts destroying the Reform with the reinstitution of the old regime. This had come about by a series of opportunistic moves by the old conservatives, alarmed at the pace of change that was gathering around the country. It was initiated by the death in June of Prince Kung, President of the military and naval forces. The Prime Minister Weng T'ung Ho should have succeeded him but the Empress, still exerting considerable influence from her so called retirement, saw to it that one of her relations should take up the position.

She then made sure that all ministers of high office dealt directly with her. With the conservative element constantly lobbying her that the Emperors' wild schemes would spell disaster for the country and that she should consider taking full control of the country's affairs once again. She declared that she would review the troops in Tientsin that autumn. The Reformers were now convinced that this was a pretext to gain the support of the army and overthrow the Emperor and so they urged him to prevent her from carrying out the review thus not giving her the opportunity to address her supporters. Furthermore they said he should surround the Summer Palace with his own guards to ensure that she could not communicate with anyone that they had not given prior approval.

Yuan Shih-k'ai was a man of outstanding ability, later he would become the President of the Chinese Republic. He was now a member of the Reform party, heavily ambitious and surrounded by a host of admirers. The

Emperor, recognising his leadership qualities, summoned him and told him of his fears and that unless immediate action was taken there would be no hope for members of the Reform party, he even felt that his own life might be at risk and certainly those at the head of the party were very exposed.

Yuan had sworn to obey the Emperor's orders and immediately brought in troops known to be loyal from Tientsin to surround the Dowagers palace, he had in the meantime received authorisation to kill Viceroy Jung Lu, the Dowager's right hand man, and then take over his office and his army. Unfortunately, sensing which way the wind was blowing, he instead dashed off to see Jung Lu and told him what actions he had been commanded to carry out. This move now put in train a series of events that would ultimately lead to disastrous consequences as he had now committed himself against Reform and on the side of reaction. Maybe it was because he felt indebted to the Dowager for his current position or that he had little faith in a young inexperienced Emperor guiding the country through an era of change. Jung Lu wasted no time in setting up protection for the Dowager Empress against the Emperor. She summoned her party elders and with her loyal troops in place a *coup d'etat* was quickly carried out. Into this maelstrom unknowingly sailed Timothy Richard, having been invited to Peking by the Emperor to act as a foreign adviser. It just so happened that on board the ship that he had taken to Peking he had met two very interesting men. One was called Yuan Chang who in two years time, during the *Siege of the Legations* in 1900 was to visit the Dowager to protest about the massacring of the foreigners, a protest that she reacted to very cooly. The act that was to cost him his life however, was when he managed somehow to intercepted her telegrams and substituted the wording from "Exterminate the foreigner" into "Protect the foreigner". His other companion was an American Chinese Dr. Yung Wing.

On hearing of his arrival in Peking K'ang Yu-Wei hastened over to tell him that the situation was deteriorating quickly, there was insurrection in the air and that he was now about to depart for Shanghai. He said that the Emperor's tutor would now be Timothy's main source of communication. Whilst in his hotel he found that the Marquis Ito was also staying there. Timothy had suggested to K'ang some months previous that Ito should be employed by the Chinese government as an advisor as he was mainly responsible for converting Japan into a modern industrial and naval power.

Before Jung Lu had managed to contact the Dowager, she had already become suspicious of the Emperor's intentions through her network of spies. When he did arrive it only confirmed what she already had assumed and he was put to task to assemble forces for her protection. Jung Lu contacted a well known semi-barbarous General – T'ung Fu-hsaing, who had a most feared and barbaric army based in Kansu. They were well known for carrying out the pillaging of the provinces, spurred on by the promise that they could keep any spoils they could lay their hands on by looting. At the same time she demanded that the Emperor arrest K'ang who she maintained was intent on poisoning his mind to act against her.

The Emperor was now panicking and sent a message to

an unsuspecting K'ang to leave for Shanghai immediately. Unaware of his danger K'ang set sail for Tientsin having first tried to board a Chinese steamer and fortuitously for him, changing his mind and then boarding a British ship. The Dowager had now reached Peking and immediately ordered K'ang's arrest. Finding out that he had already departed she sent coded messages, first to Chefoo where the boat would call en route, and also to Shanghai instructing that he be arrested and instantly decapitated. As the ship docked in Chefoo, K'ang innocently walked along the beach carrying out his hobby of collecting unusual sea shells. He was saved only by the fact that the one person who could decode the telegram had disembarked before him. At Shanghai it was different; the authorities had received the coded message and were ready to board the ship on its arrival. The British in the meantime had also, through their spy network, managed to obtain and decipher the telegram and were very concerned on the international ramifications that could arise from his arrest in a port that was under foreign control. The British Consul took a fast boat to Woosung to meet the British steamer at its next port of call to make sure that K'ang was advised and recommended that he should carry out a transfer to a P. & O. steamer and sail on to Hong Kong. This was swiftly carried out and K'ang, soon after landing made his way to Europe to avoid the clutches of the Dowager.

Before all of this took place Timothy had been visited by the Emperor's tutor who wanted to tell him that His Majesty wished him to attend an audience on the 23rd September. This never took place as the coup intervened.

The Marquis Ito on hearing that Yuan had jumped ship, stated that without control of the army the Emperor was powerless and packed his bags and left. The Dowager was now acting with great speed and swept into Peking, seized the Emperor, and held him on a small island in the Palace lake. All this happened at exactly the time that Timothy was scheduled to meet the Emperor. The Dowager had now seized control and ostensibly the Emperor was a prisoner serving a life sentence. Now further bad news reached Timothy, an edict was being formulated for the arrest of his two assistants..

Measures were now being taken to enable them and the Emperor to survive together with their faithful cohorts who were all in greater danger and could be killed at a moments notice. Contact was made with all the Christian ministers and the foreign embassies. Timothy made his way to Tientsin, anything to distance himself from the epicentre of revolt in Peking. There he met the minister of the British Legation. Meeting him he urged that every effort should be made to save the Emperor and the lives of the Reformers. To his disappointment he discovered that the minister, freshly arrived, was totally unacquainted with the language or any of the influential people and almost totally ignorant of the situation that now befell them and had little or no knowledge of Timothy's potential influence.

On 21st September the city gates of Tientsin were closed, all trains stopped and a search carried out for the leading Reformers. Most Reformers were now hastily boarding as many steamers in the harbour as possible – most trying to get to Japan whilst others made for Macao and even America. Six notable Reformers were caught and executed without a trial. One of these was the son of the Commissioner who at the time was so anti foreign that he had instigated the "Opium War". He had been refused permission to speak but he managed to break free and shouted to the watching crowd that reformers in other lands had died for their cause and that he was only too willing to do the same for China. He was hastily bustled away and never seen again. His wife, hearing of his execution committed suicide. Others were banished to Kashgar, the equivalent of modern day Siberia. They were not to suffer for too long as the Boxers found them two years later and murdered them all. Most went to ground in the country. Wang Chao, a close personal friend of the Rev. George Owen who was also close to Timothy had fled to Japan. A year later a Buddhist priest knocked on Timothy's door and, refusing to give him his card, traced on Timothy's hand his name – Wang Chao- and then disappeared just as mysteriously into the night.

On the 4th June 1899 an edict appeared in the Emperor's name stating that due to ill health he was obliged to abdicate. Most of the population realised that this was the hand of the Dowager, but as she was now all-powerful no one dared to blatantly oppose these actions even though there was a strong undercurrent of dissent. The Dowager, sensing that she was not carrying the population's approval with the forced abdication, made public that he was still the Emperor, omitting that it was only in name and that she had assumed all Imperial authority.

All along Timothy had warned the Reformers about

acting with undue haste and how it might trigger a reaction with the conservative forces in the old government. He had tried to get them to adopt a slower approach to change and to gradually convince the Dowager, as they had done the Emperor, of the need for change, but it was not to be. Thus ended the first Reform Movement

Timothy now wrote to those in exile précising the problem.

"The Manchus refuse the help of friendly foreigners.

The Mandarins are intent on insulting those from the west but at the same time want to learn about modern military and naval affairs, they want to learn about mining technology but only so that they can create enough wealth and power to drive these same foreigners from their land. If nations only seek their own national interests first then no matter how great they are they cannot last very long."

19 – The Boxer Revolution

With the fall of the Reform movement, the Empress Dowager was now convinced that she could overcome all opposition with the use of her army. The collapse of Reform let loose an avalanche of Boxer revolutions and miseries – forces that would ultimately overthrow the dynasty.

She now abrogated all of the Reform Decrees but what she hadn't realised was that the impetus of the movement had established many modern schools – mostly carried out by transforming Buddhist temples into educational establishments. This had been managed due to the domination of Confucianism which meant that it was able to further increase its grip over its rivals. Those in control preferred to seize the property of its rivals rather than raise the status of the educational work of China's Great Sage, an act that many thought contrary to his teachings. So it was that the Dowager and her followers in Peking became increasingly reactionary whilst the country as a whole still carried undercurrents of progressive thought that helped to keep the Boxer upheaval concentrated in a few areas.

Timothy was now aware that the threats that others had perceived to be against him were being diluted; from what source within the governing body he did not know. The S.D.K. Committee in the summer of 1899 felt it was safe enough to send him to Peking to see what influence he could bring to bear on the Government to establish an organised scheme of education in China. Their antenna had detected that there was still an element in the Government that wanted progress, but not at the speed desired by the Reformers. His mandate was to find out whether, and by what method, such a scheme of education could be advanced, and to what extent the S.D.K. could assist in providing literature. Sir Robert Hart, the President of the Society, was very pessimistic about the enterprise as he thought that the government would see this as another attempt at reform and he advised against any approach to high officials.

Timothy however, ignored this and following his instinct did see a few of them. One of these was a man called Chou Fu. He later became Governor of Shantung and Viceroy at Nanking. The two formed an immediate bond and spent many hours discussing China's problems and relations with the outside world and he also declaring that he had a profound interest in Christianity. He would later show this kinship by saving the lives missionaries in Szechuan riots [The Cloudy Province] in 1900.

With reactionaries in power Timothy was under no illusion that anti-foreign feelings would rise again. This was further fuelled by foreign aggression that helped to stoke the fire of their anger. Fanatics were now roaming the corridors of power demanding the expulsion of all foreigners. Fortunately they were neither organised nor of a particularly high intellect and the Manchu's continued to tread the path of chaotic implementation to any whim that crossed their mind. In order to form a militia that could be employed for national defence a Manchu – K'ang

Yi, that Timothy had known in Shansi, decided that if he was to be able to equip and train these troops, with the authorisation of the Empress Dowager, he should travel through the richest parts of China and extract as many levies as possible. He soon became known as the "Great Extortioner" and through his actions gradually eroded any positive feelings towards the government.

Meanwhile, the foreign aggression mounted as the Germans in Shantung started to stoke up the Boxer mob's anti foreigner feelings. It all started around the murder of two Roman Catholic priests in 1897. France had declared itself the protector of all Roman Catholic missionaries but these two missionaries were German and being impatient with the French reaction to these murders Germany took things into its own hands and taking the opportunity to intervene seized the port of T'sing –tao, a port the Chinese unfortunately had earmarked as a future naval base. The Chinese unaware of the German intentions, were carrying out drill practice on the parade ground and thinking that the Germans had landed to carry out a similar task, offered them their facility to practice on! To the Chinese surprise, the German's swiftly occupied the area, Prince Henry was dispatched in connection with this move following the Kaisers well publicised "Mailed Fist " policy This term for armed force or superior might is translated from the German first used in 1897 by, Kaiser William II in a speech in which he said, 'But should any one essay to detract from our just rights or to injure us, then up and at him with your mailed fist'. At first the expression *mailed fist* was used to describe Germany's aggressive foreign policy, then it was used for similar behaviour by other countries, and from there spread to general use. China was forced to yield to all of Germany's demands, at the same time Russia forced the Chinese to grant a lease on Port Arthur, at that time their most important naval port, Great Britain was also seeking and obtained expansion in Shantung, France was pressing for expansion in the south and even Italy, with little or no current interests was seeking a slice of the action by trying to obtain the only remaining suitable naval base of San-mun Bay. Back in Europe diplomats were locked behind doors secretly dividing China up into segments that they could control, as they would do in Arabia later on.

Now in 1900 all this pent up hatred started to drive the Reformers and the reactionary Boxers into a mutual desire to drive these unwelcome people back into the sea, "back to where they had come from". The Boxers, [the name was derived from their adherence to traditional boxing and martial arts, which they were convinced protected them from bullets]. Originally a banned Taoist secret society, they were adept at stoking up the feelings of the populace to achieve their prime objective – the overthrow of the hated Manchu Qing dynasty- and the restoration of the native Ming dynasty. At this time they were blaming famines on the government, promoting anti German feeling was easily achieved due to their perceived aggression. Convincing the people that foreign imports such as railways, telegraphs and certain medicines were upsetting the guardian spirits and were helping to bring about the spate of natural tragic outcomes that occurred regularly was also quite easily achieved. From starting as an anti dynastic movement it morphed into an anti-foreign and anti – Christian movement mobilising the youth in the country to spearhead change. The Dowager Empress now cunningly co-opted the Boxers, convincing them that their ultimate goals were the same "Exterminate the Foreigner" was the war cry but with tag "Uphold the Dynasty" added on. They even gained the support of the main women's reactionary movement – The Red Lantern Society. The storm clouds were gathering, unfortunately the various legations were blind and deaf to gathering undercurrent of revolution.

One man, Dr. Arthur Smith whose antenna was particularly sensitive to the changing politics did try to warn the American Legation in Peking but these were ignored. Timothy however, who felt the same as Smith, took his report with him to the Executive of the Ecumenical Committee in New York to warn them of the dangers that all foreigners faced in China. Again this information was not taken on board, the Committee did not want to get involved in politics. He then went on to Washington where his exhortations were given a little recognition until very slowly the politicians began to realise that here was a man who had a very important message not only that the safety of the missions was at stake but also peace in that part of the world. He was asked to see the President of the Senate, John Hoar who listened but explained that nothing could be done without the support of two thirds of the Senate plus that of the major cities with New York being the most influential. He moved swiftly on to that city meeting the Chairman of the Chamber of Commerce who told him that nothing short of a massacre could justify any further action. Downhearted he returned to China via Japan and no sooner had he landed than he receive the first of many telegrams informing him that the massacres had in deed begun. He also learnt that his fellow missionaries in Shantung had narrowly escaped death by being smuggled out in carts by sympathisers. Peking was now cut off from the outside world as the mob rampaged through the cities and countryside. Thinking what to do next, when his boat reached Kobe, its next port of call, he telegraphed the British Consul-General in Shanghai advising that Lord Salisbury should announce to the Viceroys and Governors of China that the British Government would hold each individual personally responsible for the safety of British subjects. Having sent the telegraph anonymously he was delighted to read in the Shanghai morning paper that his exact words had been acted upon.

Using this information he sent a wire to his mission in Si-an, the capital of Shensi, repeating the Reuters telegram knowing full well that it would be read *en route* and its contents passed on to the Chinese governors. Unfortunately it was too late to save the lives of those killed by Yu Hsein the autocratic Manchu Governor of Shansi who had already killed all of the Protestant and Catholic missionaries. It was not too late for the Manchu Governor of Shensi to decide on his own actions. He did not tell anyone of the Dowager Duchess's orders that he had received. Keeping quiet for a few vital days, he sent soldiers to escort all those missionaries in his province to safety out of his area and on to Hankow, a city first visited by Europeans in 1858 when Lord Elgin in H.M.S. Furious landed and chose the site for a British settlement. On hearing this Timothy was just in time to prevent the German troops from burning down the residence of another friendly Governor in Peking which, had it happened would have had major implications. The Governor, Tuan Fang was in residence at the time and had for months risked his life to save those that he could. He became a firm ally of Timothy's and was ultimately to achieve the position of Viceroy of Nanking. Again, this was not to last as when the Revolution did finally sweep through the country, he was assassinated by soldiers from his own army. Timothy felt greatly for the loss of so many of his friends and wondered if things could have been different had he stayed in Shansi province, an area where he had lived so long and dearly loved. He had known and worked with many of those who held high office and who now supported the Boxer cause and felt that perhaps he could have negotiated a better outcome with them.

When the Empress Dowager's telegram did arrive with the orders to exterminate all foreigners, free rein was given to all subordinate Chinese officials to carry them out and so those who twenty years earlier had spent their lives saving thousands of starving people were now murdered, often in a most brutal fashion guaranteed to give a slow lingering death.

Shansi was particularly hard hit, led by Yu Hsein who supervised the murder of over 159 missionaries, women and children included, some by his own hand. Thousands of Christians were put to death. The Boxers now spread throughout the North of China killing any Chinese converts and foreign missionaries that they came across. Fortunately, in the south the local mandarins who disapproved of the xenophobic policies being pursued by the Empress Dowager's court managed to shield most of the very vulnerable members around. Timothy was fortunate; having made many friends in the area he was better protected than most. The Empress Dowager now upped the anti on June 21st, issuing a declaration of war against all foreign powers as she stated "The foreigners have been aggressive towards us, infringed upon our territorial integrity, trampled our people under their feet. They oppress our people and blaspheme our gods. The common people suffer greatly at their hands and each one of them is vengeful. Thus it is that the brave followers of the Boxers have been burning churches and killing Christians. The green light had now been given to destroy the foreign legations in Peking.

The Western powers reaction was to exact revenge in exactly the same manner and of similar proportion by giving no quarter. The German Emperor declared that when Germany extracted its revenge no prisoners were to be taken and that German leadership must be remembered by crushing those who dared to resist. Out of the foreign aggression, chiefly made by the Germans, the ignorance, prejudice and superstition of the Chinese came to the fore and the legations were besieged and destroyed with thousands of people slaughtered and Peking left ruined. Ultimately in retaliation the western powers imposed crippling indemnities on China so that it never fully recovered economically or politically, the scene was now set for the next revolution in 1911.

20 – Education and a Return to Normality

Shansi was still a hotbed of revolution and in 1901 Prince Ch'ing and Viceroy Li Hung Chang invited Timothy to travel north and assist in quelling the eruption of the constant riots and mob rule in the area. The task was not easy as the Western Allies had avenged the Boxer massacres by executing their leaders and the Chinese population was in fear as they were convinced that any expeditionary force arriving would perform similar acts of retribution. The leaders of the Shansi province sent an appeal to Timothy to find some way around any potential conflict. He told them in no uncertain terms that unlike other religions he was not intent on reparation, missionaries' lives should not be exchanged for dollars as it would and had led to extreme feelings of resentment. Instead he proposed that a fine be imposed on the province, payment to be spread over ten years, and that this sum be used to establish a university based on western lines to improve the knowledge of young men on the ways of the modern world outside China.

This was a masterstroke as he appeared to the West to impose some hardship on an area that had acted so barbarously, whilst at the same time showing the local Chinese that he had no long-term ill feeling towards them and was prepared to give them a chance to change and improve their lives. He was prepared to forgive the stoning to death of women and children, the beheading of them and the burning of families in their houses; he recognised that there was a difference of perception between the Christian and non-Christian communities but more importantly to recognise that China was to all intents and purposes still locked into the Middle Ages. He needed a vehicle to help fast track them out of this self-imposed exile. He found that there was no regret from the masses for the massacres of, as they saw them, foreign barbarians so that tit for tat execution of their leaders would only have inflamed their prejudices, heavy fines would have increased still further the residual resentment towards the foreigner, it seemed that the only way out was through education, first of the bright young people eager for change and then spreading to the mass education of the populace.

Timothy negotiated a fine of 50,000 taels per year to run for ten years, a sum that was easily affordable for such a large province. He made sure that it was broadcast that none of this money would go out of the province and that all would be ploughed into higher education. The proposal was immediately taken up by the academics who set about appointing professors, arranging the curriculum and making sure that all spending was in Timothy's hands and not diverted to any corrupt official. Timothy announced that he would lead his project for the whole period of the ten year fine after which the control would pass to the Shansi Government.

The Chinese Government was taking a close interest in this development and very quickly proposed that similar programmes should be rolled out across the country. With the obvious shortage of competent teachers but, more importantly, there was a total lack of students with the required elementary education to understand modern principles so the portents were not good. There were also forces of opposition to overcome from the conservative elements within China. Where mismanagement could be created, it was, where chaotic organisation could be employed, it was and where subversive activities could be employed, they were. Timothy still had duties to carry out in Shanghai and whilst away found out that a rival Chinese controlled university was being proposed in Shansi. This was to be under an anti-foreign official who opposed in every way the principles of Timothy's educational foundation. As he was against the waste of resources in establishing more than one university in one city he returned from Shanghai to negotiate with the Governor of the province to amalgamate the two institutions, as they were both at this stage embryonic. He proposed that it would be more efficient to unite the two into one university with two departments. The Conservative element in their department could teach Chinese learning; while in the other, under foreign direction, Western learning could be taught. This negated the need for two sets of professors, apparatus and buildings. After prolonged deliberations this proposal was accepted and regulations drawn up forming the structure in these two departments, a Chinese department for Chinese studies under Chinese control, and a Western department for Western subjects under Timothy's control. During these negotiations the conservative officials thought they could get one over Timothy as they were convinced that the mature students who had already matriculated would support them, but they had miscalculated the progressive nature of younger minds and on a vote of these students 68 were in favour of change and only 13 were against. On the other hand others thought Timothy had thrown away a golden opportunity to found a definitive Christian university based on the martyrdom of so many devout missionaries. Timothy, ever the pragmatist, had to recognise the fact that you could not set up such an organisation with a limited amount of Christian students and to compel an entire body of non Christian students to submit to Christian propaganda in an institution established by non-Christian provincial funds. It would be open to any accusation of immorality. Moreover he recognised that a rival institution backed by an anti foreign government full of like-minded officials would destroy any spirit of friendship that could be kindled. He had already been exposed to officials attempting to ban any form of western teaching in the university, an attempt that he wholeheartedly refused to agree with. At one stage he was exposed to an eight-hour argument with a Chinese intellectual who tried to convince him that no form of Christianity should be on the curriculum. Mentally exhausted he retired to a small anti room where he rested and then re gathered his thoughts. Going back to the discussion he told the man that the question of religious liberty had been agreed to by China in several treaties with foreign nations. If the Governor had now received fresh instructions to supersede all of these treaties and could show him proof, then he might consider entering into a discussion forbidding Christian and western teachings. No more was heard on the subject again.

To help him, Timothy installed Dr. Moir Duncan as First Principal to establish and run the university on a multi faith basis. This brought even more support for Timothy, as the leaders of various religions that might be in the minority in certain areas would provide support even though they were in the majority in other areas.

They now embarked on a tour of the local districts giving lectures and drumming up interest in the embryo university. Such was the interest in some towns that they could not find buildings big enough to hold the audiences. They now turned their attention to their own facilities. Dr. Duncan was in charge of planning and building of the University infrastructure. Governor Ts'en lent them the best building in the city for the temporary use of the university. On the day of the handover Timothy found that the very man he had appointed to head the Chinese department had travelled to Peking to claim that Ts'en was ignoring Chinese rights by handing everything over to Timothy. Fortunately Ts'en was made of stern stuff and had a reputation for being honest and straightforward, not only that he was on the right side of the Empress Dowager as he had supported her during her flight from Peking. He had a fearsome reputation for decapitating anyone found guilty of corruption or from extorting money from those that could least afford it. His promotion was rapid with several Viceroyalties to his credit, each time his detractors were hoping that he was promoted beyond his level of competence.

This head of department who was determined to undermine Timothy's authority now had totally miscalculated Ts'en's frame of mind, who on hearing his accusations, told him to hand over everything in the Chinese department of the university and leave the city instantly. Ts'en was now a very angry man and warned all that if they tried to work in any subversive manner he would not deal with them so lightly, his officials were so frightened of his reaction that they dared not plead the head of departments case.

That afternoon a farewell dinner was prepared for Timothy's departure for Peking. At the end of the meal Timothy rose to thank Ts'en for his support, kindness and to congratulate the province on having a Governor that had accomplished two major tasks, the like of which had not been seen in Shansi before – the founding of a modern university and the start of a railway to cross the province. The Governor then stood up and told all the dignitaries there that both of these projects were due to Timothy – he had merely sanctioned them. Timothy some years previous had told the Chinese government that the only way to unite the country was by building railways. In that way communication would swift, troubles such as famine could quickly be brought under control, wealth would be created from accessing the vast natural resources and administration could be standardised. All of this he was convinced had been seen in Europe and more recently in India where as a result of the railway networks e central control of vast areas of land had brought stability and economic progress. He told them that in Britain it had taken only thirty years to establish a nationwide network and that even before he had come to China it was possible to journey across the country through links to all the major industrial cities, it was a fact that it was industry that drove mass communication. The regulations for the new university were duly signed and sent to Peking where the contracts were then issued in September 1902 for the erection of the first buildings. These were the most modern in China and nothing on this scale had been seen before. The two departments were built on a large site within Shansi city close to the southern wall. The Western college comprised a large assembly hall, which could double as an examination hall, a library, gymnasium, museum, offices and reception rooms together with lecture rooms and laboratories. On top of this each school had its own rooms, law, languages, literature, history were in one building; physics in another whilst chemistry, mining and civil engineering were in another. The scope and breadth of learning that would come from this facility astounded the conservative elements. All of the buildings were Chinese in style and made as simple and inexpensive as possible. The whole complex was lit by electricity and heated with modern boilers which had been transported on mules from Tientsin.

Now the focus turned to filling these facilities with students. Bearing in mind that few people let alone potential students knew what the terms "physics", "chemistry" or even mining engineering stood for. On top of that most people only knew the language of their area, so Timothy and Duncan embarked on a daring strategy of establishing the principle of fast track learning based on an idea of Timothy's. As there were no students that spoke English and no professors to be had that understood Chinese they employed interpreters from the main coastal ports. This was the best halfway house as these men did not understand the subjects being taught nor did they speak the local language but they could interpret the lectures of the Western professors into Mandarin, which was generally understood and this went on until the professors had attained fluency in speaking Chinese or the students could understand English.

Starting with the most elementary content of the subjects it was not long before the hand picked students displayed their greater intellectual capabilities by soaking up the information at a rapid rate. They were generally graduates with either an M.A. or B.A. and came from all over the province. After three years the majority had obtained an M.A. in their new curriculum. Specialised courses lasting four years then followed for the high achievers in subjects such as law, physics and chemistry, or mining and civil engineering. The finals took place in Peking where those that were successful were awarded a Doctorate. Such was the success of this enterprise that the Provincial Government bore the expense of sending the most successful students to England for a further five years study. Thus Shansi could boast that it had more Chinese students in England than all the other Chinese universities together.

On its foundation it soon became clear that one of the weak points was the lack of text and reference books. One major problem that rose was when technical or modern words were used previous translators had and still did, put their own interpretation as to what they thought it meant. The way around this was the establishment of a board of Terminology in Peking where all new words had to be submitted and given an official description. Timothy had anticipated this and Shansi University already had a translation department working in close conjunction with Shanghai University – this information was also fed to Japan via one of his assistants. From this a stream of technical journals and text books, emerged from the printing presses on subjects such as mathematics, botany, mineralogy, zoology, physiology, physics, teaching; also atlases, geographical maps and copies of the important tracts that were used for teaching in the West. The cost of carrying out this tremendous task was almost crippling and when Timothy told a Viceroy friend of his that the University could only afford to pump 10,000 taels per annum he immediately responded that he would match it and get the Minister of Education to do likewise.

Timothy's plan for the university soon became the model for the Chinese Empire. When he had started there was no plan for national education yet within no time at all an edict had been issued to establish a modern university in each provincial capital – this sadly, as with many other of his progressive ideas did not reach its full potential as the 1911 revolution curtailed nearly all of these. However, the enthusiasm for modern education had spread like a wave over China and then even further into Japan where Chinese students would also travel to expand their learning. Japan seized on this new opportunity faster than China as they were much more organised, China stumbled on being slow to adapt and lacked the thoroughness that their near neighbours employed from the start. In this respect China and Britain shared one thing in common – a relaxed attitude to things shown by the expressions "not far wrong" or "somewhere about" in Chinese or adding the expression "ish" to time or actions in Britain.

In 1902 the Empress appointed an elderly scholar, Chang, to write a report on how to modernise the education system. This report modelled itself on the system used in Japan mainly because the Viceroy knew no foreign language but had access to the Japanese system this being easier to understand due to the commonality of the written form with Chinese. Thus another chance was missed to bring the benefits of modern western learning to China, it also carried on exposing the younger graduates to the old school methods and practices. Instead of fast tracking these younger people on four year courses, they followed the Japanese practice of sixteen years which meant that any rising new talent was isolated for this period of time, there was no interim shorter timescale system to allow graduates to bring what they had learnt to benefit others.

Timothy now entered into a difficult period. In March 1903 it was found that his wife, Mary, was suffering from cancer. In spite of an operation carried out in Shanghai she never recovered and died the following July. He had now lost his major inspiration as the two of them fed off each other for ideas and then together they made sure that they were implemented. She criticised him when he assumed that others would follow him with same zeal and dedication and always followed up to make sure that everything was in place and followed through. At her funeral, the cemetery chapel was full with friends from all stations of life both European, Chinese and

Japanese. He also now had to look after the welfare of his four daughters.

In 1904 war broke out between Russia and Japan. With China caught in the middle hiding behind an outdated army and navy. Russia, they feared the most and Japan they despised the most. Their battles were fought mostly on Chinese territory with each of these two countries occupying and claiming towns and villages. To Timothy came Tao-t'ai who had assisted him in founding the university and to whom he naturally felt obliged to help. Together they formed the International Red Cross Society in China as a means of helping all those caught up and displaced in the hostilities. This was no easy task, as although the Chinese had secured the funds, the Russians and Japanese would in no way co-operate. Timothy now tried another tack. He had a friend, James Webster, who was the recognised expert on Manchuria and more importantly, knew the Russian General in charge of the army. Together they obtained the permission to send relief parcels of food, medicine and clothing plus substantial amounts of money together with medical staff. Timothy put the Japanese General in an invidious position by telling him that if he withheld his consent then he would broadcast his name and any negative actions throughout the world via the major places of worship and government. Then in 1907, his trusted friend Dr. Duncan died at the age of forty-five.

The first Contingent of Shansi Students
leaving for England
Dressed uncomfortably in European costume

This meant more work for him until he was able to appoint an acting principal at Shansi University. The man he chose was Professor Loius Bevan and after a year Professor Soothill was made Principal. The University was now teeming with academic life with over 300 students in residence, the first batch of twenty five had already been sent to study mining and railway engineering in England and at the same time the province was planning for the construction of its first railway, this was being done by Belgian engineers. Further progress at the University was made by commencing specialised courses in law, physics and chemistry. To check the progress Timothy visited Shansi at the start of 1908 where two thousand students from the province attended to hear him speak, all of these students having been taught by graduates from Shansi.

He would not visit Shansi university again until 1910 where in his speech he declared to all in attendance that rather than wait for the original agreed term he would hand over the control of university immediately as all the reforms he had planned were now firmly in place. The success of the university was now unrivalled in the country. It now proved capable of taking mature men, teaching them the alphabet, the first steps in mathematics and science and turn them into scholars within seven years. Jealousy still reigned in Peking as they had not been able to equal these results. Shortly after the handover the central government installed a German trained superintendent to run the whole complex and he decided to completely change the system of running the Western department. Germany was desperate to extend its influence in the region and was only too willing to put money into the right pockets to achieve this. It used all of its political cunning to achieve its aims and got what it wanted, but justice prevailed, the university was finally handed over in June 1911 and all of the German efforts came to nothing as the Xinhai revolution broke out in October. The newly installed Governor of the region was assassinated and a large part of the city destroyed. The revolution was motivated by anger at corruption in the Qing government, frustration with the government's inability to restrain the interventions of foreign powers, and the majority Han Chinese's resentment toward a government dominated by an ethnic minority; the Manchus.The revolution set up a weak provisional central government over a politically fragmented country. Reactionaries briefly and abortively restored the monarchy twice, leading to a period of military rule. Though the revolution concluded on February 12, 1912, when the Republic formally replaced the Qing Dynasty,

Timothy's wife, a former teacher, had gone around the university buildings putting up notices highlighting its achievements and goals and in consequence none of the buildings were touched, however in the ensuing chaos the Revolution meant that there was no structured government as things gradually deteriorated students and professors melted away together with the systems that had been put in place. Timothy was fortunate, he had around him a network of allies who made sure that he was well informed of any possible hostility that might be directed against him – even better they made sure that any acts of aggression that could have come his way were countered before they flared out of control.

Shansi University in the early 1900's

Shansi University's influence did not fade so fast and its effect on the country could still be seen, felt and noted by subsequent visitors from Britain and America. What had once been a large opium poppy growing area had been cleared of the drug and famine was no longer a major problem. The population was now largely doing meaningful work producing surpluses off the land which were in turn being sold to neighbouring provinces.

21 – Revolution and Retrenchment

The Xinhai or Chinese Revolution of 1911 pitted the Chinese Revolutionary Army against the Imperial Forces of the Qing Dynasty. It was motivated as stated before by the general anger at the corruption of the Qing's, their apparent inability to stop the onward march of foreign powers and also resentment at being controlled by an ethnic minority – the Manchus. From 1901 the Empress Dowager, who had been brought back to power by the clever manipulations of Viceroy Jung Lu, had done a complete about turn, gained control, started at last to issue edicts to enable China to modernise its education system and open modern schools much to the relief of the suppressed progressive elements. Exposure to Western law and politics made them realise how much had been lost in the past. All native schools were converted to Western style learning, all suitable and able men were sent abroad, the Emperor surprising the Manchus by urging the princes to travel abroad when the law at the time forbid them to travel any more than forty Li from Peking or to sleep outside the city. He sent his brother Prince Chun to Germany to apologise for the murder of the German minister whilst Prince Tsai'Chen represented him at the Coronation of King Edward VII. The next cultural shift was the banning of the common practice of foot binding, a custom that Timothy's wife had been determined to end, although it has to be said that this was never a Manchu custom[people would often remark on the enormous size of her feet]. It was carried out by women on all social levels consequently it was rare to see anywhere in the country a shoe exceeding four inches in length. The women would hobble about on their heels always maintaining that they could walk for long distances. Large feet were considered vile and reduced their chance of marriage. The consequences of this practice could be ulceration and gangrene, often seen by the number of amputees moving around on crutches There was no defining age for starting this process it was usually done when girls were about three to five years old – the later they started the more painful it would become to carry out. The process entailed doubling four toes under the foot with the big toe laid on top. This was then tightly bandaged so that when adult there was a distinct cleft across the sole of the foot between the heel and toes which by then had been forced together. She would then have to carry out this binding process every day of her life.

The progress from 1900 on the development of the telegraph and the expansion of the railway network were all due to Timothy's constant lobbying, now too late, the Empress Dowager took up the cudgel for promoting these modern activities. At this time Timothy had sat down with the new head of Government to try to persuade the country to take up the gold standard rather than have a silver based economy since the quality of silver was not controlled and varied from province to province.

The actual revolution came as a surprise to many, in fact its main proponent Dr. Sun Yat-sen wasn't even in the country when it happened! Dr. Sun and Yuan Shih-k'ai were the two main protagonists in this event. Sun had spent many years of his life trying to undermine the authority of the throne. A reward [£100,000] for his capture had been circulated for some time such was the fear he inspired amongst those in power. Dr. Sun knew Timothy well and had met him in London where he thanked him for all the relief work he done during the famine years of the 1860's. Sun had in 1896 been tricked into entering the Chinese Legation in London and held prisoner in a cell on the top floor whilst the Chinese made arrangements to smuggle him out of the country. Somehow the Foreign Office came to hear of it and put pressure on the Chinese for his release. From then on Sun was determined to carry out in whatever format, printed or verbal, an attack on the Manchus, advocating their replacement by any form of alternative government. Timothy desperately tried to moderate his opinion but it was to no avail and ultimately he had to part company from Sun declaring that his radical ideas for a change in government without a simultaneous plan for the smooth transfer of rule did not fit in with his personal philosophy and would result in chaos and bloodshed.

Sun now carried his ideas abroad trying to persuade the Americans and French to help him set up a South China Republic. All of this was to no avail until he set foot in Japan where he found one or two sympathetic ears in government and consequently had no trouble in stirring up the radical element amongst the thousands of students who had now based themselves there for civil and military education. These men then grouped themselves and infiltrated their way back to the mainland where they set about organising small units to carry out two tasks – a] to arm China against foreign takeover and b] to destroy the Manchu hold on power.

In 1908 two events happened that undermined the hold of the Qing dynasty. Almost simultaneously the Empress Dowager Cixi and the Emperor died within weeks of each other. The legacy of Cixi's refusal to back the Emperor with his plans of reform and instead dethrone him had given Sun the mandate he desired and the opportunity to organise a private voluntary army. A child Emperor was installed on the throne with his father, the brother of the late Emperor as regent, to try and achieve some sense of continuity. Sensing that their days were numbered with such a weak ruling body, the Manchus' attempted to secure even more power in government and to fill their pockets with whatever riches they could get their hands on. Thus they further alienated themselves from their previous supporters.

The Revolution started in 1911, spearheaded by a group of Japanese trained military officers who had returned to Wuchang, in Central China and had kept in contact with the other revolutionary students spread throughout the land. The Manchu garrisons were now horribly exposed without adequate leadership or modern military equipment. Over fifteen thousand people, including women and children were butchered in Si-an-fu alone and countless others in the provincial capitals.

Yuan Shih-k'ai the Manchus strongest supporter [previously mentioned as having been the Emperor's right hand man who's allegiance was overridden by his loyalty to Cixi] had been forced to retire. The Manchu princes having to humble themselves by begging him to return to office now lost precious time. Had he still been in a powerful position the uprising could have been quelled very quickly by his deployment of a loyal army, now he set about achieving a victory over the republicans. To avoid bloodshed and to make sure his own position was secure against a background of Manchu distrust, he agreed to terms, which involved the abdication of the Emperor and the establishment of a Republic encapsulating China, Manchuria, Mongolia, Turkestan and Tibet.

Sun hurried back from London as the Revolution took hold, becoming Provisional President of the Republic and making Yuan, Prime Minister in December.. He soon realised that he did not have the necessary experience and immediately resigned so that Yuan could take over as President. It was a very fluid and ever changing situation with hardly anyone knowing who was in charge. Timothy was offering advice to Sun during this time pointing out that whilst Yuan was probably the most experienced statesman he did not have the necessary backing or knowledge of those that actually ran the country.

Sun was given the post of Director – General of Railways, a task at which he failed miserably to carry out with any sense of achievement. During his brief term of Presidency he had managed to install officers capable of even greater corruption than had been seen before. The resultant disorder meant that any cohesion that had existed in the running of the country soon fell to pieces, which meant that Yuan had to quickly reform and strengthen the Republican army to avoid total disintegration. To do this funding was required and

Yuan recklessly arranged for loans. Sun now declared his total disagreement with this course of action – even if it was short term. He started to sound out his contacts abroad to back him, clearly feeling that such an act was unconstitutional. Once again Timothy was approached to try and mediate in this schism. Sitting with Sun he was handed a proof of the protest poster that was going to be posted around the land and abroad. Timothy pleaded with him not to proceed with this course of action, as he could not carry out this action safely in China. From then on Sun's career was that of an exile. He tried to lead another revolt in 1913 but together with his fellow conspirators fled to Japan, making sure that they had amassed enough of a fortune to live comfortably. Yuan's unconstitutional act in the meantime had in fact brought some stability to the country and he wisely invited back the exiled Reformers K'ang and Liang both of whom were perhaps more in favour of a Constitutional Monarchy than with a Republic. K'ang refused to take up any form of high office but Liang became head of the department of Justice and kept in constant contact for advice with Timothy up to their final meeting in 1912.

China was now in limbo. Cohesive development was not now possible. Educational progress ground to a halt a result of which meant that Missions were once again becoming increasingly popular as parents tried to enhance the education of their children. In 1912 Timothy went to the Baptist Mission Conference in Ch'ing-chou-fu where he had laid the foundations of his movement some forty years previously. After the event he was approached by a group of non-Christians who asked if they could borrow the facility so that a public meeting could be held to thank them for all the changes that they had introduced. All religions attended teachers and scholars and a military band assembled, officials made speeches turning it into a very happy and relaxed occasion.

Timothy had by now also become Chairman of a group, leading inter religious and denominational discussions. From this sprang a movement in Shanghai where Taoists, Buddhists and other minority religions began holding meetings where they would all discuss just one topic and how they saw it and how it affected them. One regular visitor was the Taoist Pope who frequently stayed with Timothy. He was due to give a lecture on one occasion but felt so nervous about delivering it to an international audience that he begged Timothy to do it for him as "it would sound so much better coming from you". All of this came to an end – World War 1 had broken out in Europe.

In 1914 Timothy visited the capital of Hunan, perhaps the most anti-foreign and anti-Christian province in China. A notorious character Chou Han oversaw the area. He had declared that any foreigner visiting his province would be killed, butchered and the pieces fed to the populace. From this province spread the anti-foreigners riots down the Yangtse valley in the 1890's. A counter offensive had taken place in the meantime with the Reform movement using nothing more than the power of the pen and whilst some missionaries did perish, the Reform movement had gradually taken hold with the building of churches, schools and hospitals.

Timothy's arrival was timed perfectly with one of the leading families converting to Christianity, however he also arrived during a severe flood. He was well received by the Governor and other officials. The Chief Buddhist Abbot called to see him with a contingent of other monks to thank him on the work he was doing to remove religious distrust and for translating into English Buddhist books, all of which helped to break down barriers of communication.

He went on to address audiences of several hundred people in other parts of the province again advocating education and science as the glue to bind not only provinces together but also bring China into contact with the rest of the world. But China was falling apart around him and he was also worried about his family living in a Europe that was also about to tear itself apart.

The Entrance to Shansi University

The Library and Clock Tower

22 – Home

Timothy had now lived in Shanghai for eleven years. One by one his daughters had left to marry and set up home with their respective partners. Only his eldest daughter had stayed behind and in 1914, when in Yokohama he married again. His new wife was Dr. Ethel Tribe whom he had known for about five years. With her he had travelled the Dutch East Indies. In Java he was delighted at the way the different tribes with different religions managed to live together he was also surprised at the large number of Chinese living there. It appeared that in recent times the Chinese were only too keen to emigrate to places that their education had suddenly opened up to them. The idea of this trip had been to help recharge his health, as he had become quite run down, an accumulation of constant travel, exposure to tropical diseases and the extreme variations of climate that he had exposed himself to. Unfortunately this sojourn did not revive him and he developed Coeliac disease which left him very weak and prone to other ailments. It meant that he was confined to bed to start with and when he did feel better he decided to go back to Japan to convalesce.

He now felt that the time had come to retire from his duties in China. Handing over the reins of administrating the Christian Literary Society [C.L.S] to a suitable nominee and with his health deteriorated still further the decision was made in 1916 to return to England.

They left Shanghai in May to travel via Canada stopping at Banff in the Rockies. There they learnt of the death of the President of China. Timothy was now determined to make it to Wales by July but he also wanted to see his daughter Mary and her family who were now farming in New Brunswick. After a few days there they returned to Montreal leaving on the 1st July on the S.S. Metagama, escorted by a cruiser across the submarine infested North Atlantic and arriving in Liverpool on the 10th July – the port he had set out from over fifty years previous.

In spite of his weakness, he made the journey to Aberystwyth where the University conferred on him its Doctorate of Laws and Logic. This was a much-delayed honour as the authorities had wanted to do it many years earlier but unfortunately Wales and China were too far apart. He was now well recognised academically having received honours from Georgia and Brown University in the USA and innumerable accolades in China.

Still wishing to be at the heart of things Timothy and his wife decided to base themselves in London and they rented a small flat in Southampton Row.

There he carried on meeting his fellow missionary workers but as he was getting weaker it was decided to move to Shepherd's Bush before securing a house in Golders Green. Here his health did improve and he spent his time reading and writing whilst his wife helped at the local hospital. His thoughts now turned on how to unite the world after the terrible war that was being waged had ended. He started to formulate a framework for establishing a League of Religions. This was the last piece of work of importance that he spent much time on, feeling very sad about the turn of events in the West and East yet still having some hope that as Europe gradually emerged from chaos, so could China.

He was now growing visibly weaker and thinner. He still managed to travel, going to Arundel at the invitation of Sir Harry Johnson and then again to Buckingham Gate to see Lord Bryce to discuss the formation of the League of Nations. He still had many Chinese visitors the most important being that of Liang Ch'I-cha'o who was visiting England accompanied by his secretary. Timothy was heartened that the first person Liang wished to see was he and he had brought him a gift of ten volumes of his own works.

Early in 1919 Timothy and his wife had decided to return to China but this was curtailed when he had to go into hospital for surgery. He was not to recover and passed away on the 17th April 1919. He was seventy-three years old and had survived famine and disease in China but all of this had gradually taken its toll his health. He was cremated in Golders Green. The quiet funeral service held with his friends Revs. Fullerton and Glover with many old friends from China in attendance plus representatives from the Chinese and Japanese Legations.

The contrast could not have been more poignant Among his own people he was almost a stranger; amongst the "strangers" of the East he was regarded with reverence – a sage who had dispensed much wisdom, charity and love without asking for anything in return.

So ended a great life that started from humble beginnings in Wales and ended quietly in London.

China was once more on the brink of closing its doors to the outside world again.

23 – Epilogue

On his final journey to Wales, Timothy visited his sister – my Grandmother – who had bought an hotel in Swansea. My father had written an account of what it was like living in that area at that time :-

"My parents acquired the Uplands Hotel in 1904 when I was nearly five years old. At that time The Uplands was a purely residential suburb of Swansea. In fact a milestone and a water trough existed on the pavement where now stands Belgrave Flats, this indicating that Swansea was one mile away. The wooden trough was subsequently replaced by an ornate red stone affair erected by the R.S.P.C.A. There were no trams on this route at that time.

The only shop was the fairly new J.T. Davies under the management of the very able Mr. Saunders. There was however, a small shop across the Uplands Hotel passageway which at one time was occupied by the celebrated John Eynon who subsequently built the bakery – confectioners across the road. I was told that the shop was the original inn, which was which was transferred to its' present site in 1854.

Around the corner in the Grove was a greengrocer owned by a Mr. Thornsby, which was well patronised, although the main shopping was done at the old Swansea Market.

Before John Gray took over the newsagents [next to the Hotel] we used to purchase our comics from "Charlie" Evans in Bryn y-Mor Road, or Morgan the Barber in Brynmill. Beechwood, Bernard Street and all that area was part of the Pantygwydr Estate and was all fields as was a small area opposite the houses later occupied by Waynes the grocers. We used to play cricket on the grassland behind the South side of Mirador Crescent.

Sketty Road was a narrow rutted country lane and I remember seeing Haley's Comet from the walled boundary of Col. Wright's Estate. I remember the first motorcar I saw which belonged to him and was driven by his chauffeur a Mr. Taylor. Mr. Walters Ffynone had a Napier car at about the same time.

The house on the corner opposite J.T. Davies was occupied by a Mr. Schank and when it became vacant before World War 1, it was occupied during the Summer as headquarters for the Militia in their dark green uniforms. This house and that of J.T. Davies had a walled garden forming two sides of what is now Gwydr Square."

References

Timothy Richard of China   William Soothill

Timothy Richard   E.W. Price Evans

Timothy Richard, China Missionary,
Statesman and Reformer   Rev. B. Reeve

Diaries of Timothy Richard

Acknowledgements

The many stories told to me by my father. I just wish that I had listened more intently to them at the time.

Bonnie, for sitting at my feet so patiently as I typed, waiting for her next walk.

Carol, my wife, for being patient and understanding.

Index